Mankind in Amnesia

Books by Immanuel Velikovsky

WORLDS IN COLLISION (1950)

AGES IN CHAOS (1952)

EARTH IN UPHEAVAL (1955)

OEDIPUS AND AKHNATON (1960)

PEOPLES OF THE SEA (1977)

RAMSES II AND HIS TIME (1978)

MANKIND IN AMNESIA (1982)

MANKIND
IN AMNESIA

Immanuel Velikovsky

DOUBLEDAY & COMPANY, INC.
Garden City, New York
1982

70207

Library of Congress Cataloging in Publication Data
Velikovsky, Immanuel, 1895–
    Mankind in amnesia.

    Includes index.
    1. Ethnopsychology.   2. Man.   3. Human behavior.
I. Title.
GN502.V44   155.8   AACR2

ISBN: 0-385-03393-1
LIBRARY OF CONGRESS CATALOG CARD NUMBER 79-7222
PRINTED IN THE UNITED STATES OF AMERICA
FIRST EDITION

To my grandchildren
Meir, Naomi, Rivka, Rafael, Carmel

FOREWORD

by

Lynn E. Rose

Professor of Philosophy,
State University of New York at Buffalo

Immanuel Velikovsky described his work on collective amnesia as follows: "*Mankind in Amnesia* has to do not only
with the past, like my other books—primarily it has to do
with the future, a future not removed by thousands or tens
of thousands of years, but the imminent future, on whose
threshold we now stand."

The subject that Immanuel Velikovsky has chosen is the
psychological condition and case history of the human race.
Virtually every aspect of human behavior, every pattern in
human history, and every article of human belief, if examined and illuminated in the light of the thesis of this
book, reveals how human thought and action have been
shaped and molded by repressed collective memories of cosmic catastrophes that befell our ancestors as recently as one
hundred generations ago.

In the section "A Collective Amnesia" of *Worlds in Collision*, published in 1950, Velikovsky outlined his principal
psychological thesis. His theory of collective amnesia explains the inability of people to look at the overwhelming
evidence of global catastrophes—from all parts of the world

—that is unequivocally there, and the unwillingness to see the implications of that evidence. Velikovsky put this as follows in *Worlds in Collision* (pp. 300–4):

> The memory of the cataclysms was erased, not because of lack of written traditions, but because of some characteristic process that later caused entire nations, together with their literate men, to read into these traditions allegories or metaphors where actually cosmic disturbances were clearly described.

For detailed accounts of the evidence of our catastrophic past one should read Velikovsky's *Worlds in Collision* and *Earth in Upheaval*.

Velikovsky wrote *Mankind in Amnesia* over the course of many years. Most of it was written in the 1950s and early 1960s, but he added sections as late as 1979, the last year of his life.

The theme of collective amnesia was so important to Velikovsky that during those many years he never failed to include it in his lectures in colleges and universities, in several cases devoting the entire lecture to the subject. He invariably stressed a vital element of his theme, which can be summarized in his own words, from Chapter II of this work: *"Disaster may come, not from another planetary collision, but from the handiwork of man himself, a victim of amnesia, in possession of thermonuclear weapons."*

Immanuel Velikovsky died November 17, 1979, at the age of eighty-four. For the reason implicit in the passage quoted just above, he considered it imperative that *Mankind in Amnesia* appear without delay. As he wrote: "For many years my work on books has demanded all my time, yet my oath of Hippocrates—to serve humanity—I will fulfill with *Mankind in Amnesia*, a work pleading for priority." It is thus the first posthumous book, of the several Velikovsky works still to be published, to be seen through the press.

Much of the work of preparing *Mankind in Amnesia* for the press has been carried out by Elisheva Velikovsky and her assistant Jan N. Sammer.

CONTENTS

PROLOGUE
THE GOOD EARTH

It has been immensely difficult for the mind of man to part with the conviction that his Earth is immovable and in the center of Creation, thus in the center of the system to which the Sun, the Moon and the planets belong, and in which the stars are without a clear purpose or design. It is possible that the dogmatic opposition to the heliocentric system of the universe would not have been so complete and adamant were it known that though the Earth is not located in the center of the system, it occupies the preferred position and possesses the optimal conditions for life and its progress.

The Sun is a blazing flame. Mercury, the planet closest to the Sun, is so hot on its illuminated side that some metals would be molten; its face is licked by solar plasma and it has only a rudiment or a vestige of an atmosphere. Venus is enshrouded in massive clouds of dust and gases and is well over 800°F. at its ground surface, equally on its lighted and shadowed sides. Its period of daylight is as long as fifty-eight terrestrial days; its night is of equal length. The ancients called it Lucifer, and it is a hell, and no life could be sustained on its surface under the dark canopy of dust. These two planets, Mercury and Venus, are situated on orbits between the Sun and Earth.

Farther in space, Mars moves on an orbit of 687 terrestrial days; its own day is nearly of the same duration as ours, and its seasons, of double length, have the same sequence as ours; but it receives only half as much heat per unit of surface as the Earth does. If there were water on Mars it would be mostly frozen, but it seems that there is none or exceedingly little. The surface of Mars is all pocked by craters; it does not have a bucolic appearance as some thought, but is a landscape of pits and crags and waste.

Between Mars and Jupiter fragments of some exploded body, numbering in the thousands, move on orbits, and some of them cross the path of Mars and even of Earth. Several of the chunks are billions of tons heavy, but none is conceivable as an abode of life.

Jupiter and Saturn, five and nine times farther from the Sun than the Earth, receive per equal area something like one twenty-fifth and one eightieth of the solar light and heat that Earth receives. Their atmospheres contain ammonia and methane; the inner conditions are unknown. These planets have recently been considered dark stars; Jupiter is a powerful source of radio signals and has a violently moving atmosphere.

Of the other two giant planets, Uranus and Neptune, we know little, but what we know does not suggest them as places fit for the creation and procreation of life, so removed are these planets from the Sun, the dispenser of light and warmth.

Our own satellite, the Moon, is a scene of desolation: spilled oceans of lava and innumerable craters, no atmosphere and no water, half a month of exposure to scorching rays of the Sun, followed with little transition by half a month of night, unprotected by an atmosphere or by clouds from the coldness of space. As against all these inhospitable surroundings, the Earth is a blessed abode. We have plentiful water. Four fifths of the planet is covered by oceans;

evaporating, the water is desalinized and is returned in rain. Rivers and lakes are distributed on all five continents; these continents are a safe area for man, a terrestrial animal, to walk.

Earth is surrounded by an atmosphere of oxygen, diluted in nitrogen, one part against four parts, so that the oxidation process—in the act of animal breathing—does not burn the tissues.

Plants live in a symbiosis with the animals—the latter consume oxygen and exhale carbon dioxide, and the former consume carbon dioxide and exhale oxygen. From the minerals of the ground, from water, air and sunshine, plants extract their food and produce their fruits, each plant on a formula of its own, and animals feed on these fruits.

The water of this planet, outside of the oceans, is partly frozen or solid, partly liquid and flowing, and partly in the state of vapor that moistens the atmosphere. The oceans are a rich abode of life (actually life is supposed to have originated there, to emerge with time and populate a land ready to accept it and give it the chance to multiply).

The Earth in its entirety is surrounded by a magnetosphere that protects it and its inhabitants from the noxiousness of cosmic rays, particles of energy hurled by the Sun and other stars with millions and billions of electron volts of charged energy. Under the cover of the magnetosphere a layer of ozone protects the Earth and its denizens from ultraviolet light—the mutation-producing spectrum of invisible light accompanying the visible light coming from the Sun. X rays coming from space are also filtered out, and meteoric dust is mostly burned out in flight through the atmosphere.

The Earth, with its atmosphere and oceans, rotates on its axis once in about twenty-four hours, and thus the alternation of day and night follows at periods convenient to the interchange of activity and rest, or nightly sleep. This measured sequence, so pleasing to us, is of much more rapid succession on the giant Jupiter, where day and night in the mean are less than five hours each. How different would be our working hours and our social activities if the entire span from rising to going to sleep were only five hours, or interchanged once in fifty-eight terrestrial days as on Venus, or at even longer intervals as on Mercury.

On the Earth, traveling in an orbit of 365 days' duration, the plants complete their cycle, and with each new circling nature regenerates; the inclination of the axis to the plane of revolution causes seasons and their sequence.

These situations and phenomena are responsible for the development of life on the planet and for its progression to presently existing forms, man included. With all his ingenuity, man has not yet succeeded in creating life from inorganic material; but nature—light and heat and other forms of energy in proper proportions applied to matter containing the element carbon—started life and developed it, discarding numerous forms but selecting others, until through many vicissitudes *homo sapiens* evolved and in a rapid progress developed arts and industries, and multiplied his interests and enjoyments, listened to tonal vibrations and created symphonies, distinguished colors and created visual art, another of his worlds of imagination. To live in comfort, he invented thousands of devices and to live in security he provided for law and its enforcement.

Man is curious about the world of nature around him and studies the chromosomes and genes, the microcosmos of molecules and atoms and subatomic particles, and the macrocosmos of stars and galaxies. He finds that there are billions of galaxies; a galaxy like the Milky Way has a hundred billion stars, and probably some of the stars have planets revolving around them—but is there a chance that conditions on them are ripe or beneficial for life and its development?

No signals have yet arrived from outer space that could be ascribed to intelligent senders; having learned how desolate Venus and Mars are, we are certain that we are the only intelligent inhabitants of the solar system, regardless of whether or not in the past other planets, possibly on different orbits, had developed life on them.

Gone forever are the little green men—the Venusians, the claimed sighting of whom was accepted as a fact by gullible people. Then there were the Martians, a breed of strange design, who existed in the fantasy of many but were detected by nobody. It is nearly seven and a half billion miles across the orbit of the farthest planet, and over twenty-five trillion miles to the next star, with the domain of our Sun stretching over an area of an equal diameter. Our solar system is meaningful, more than for anything else, as the abode of man. Nature is certainly generous and free-spending to allow all this space for the luxury of creating man, but the actual space he occupies is immeasurably small in that area delineated by the Sun's dominion—a planet eight thousand miles across. In our age, man circled this ball of rock, with its oceans and atmosphere, in ninety minutes of travel. Light, if traveling in a circle, would go around the Earth eight times in a single second, and this is our portion of the universe.

A world so puny in so large a space—but in the optimal portion of that space: are we not lucky? The question is self-negating because we would not be here if the conditions were not so beautifully arranged. It may appear that Providence must be behind the plan and that the conditions that prevail on Earth now must have been prearranged and existing from the beginning of time, at least from the first stage in the development of the solar system. But the frightening fact is that the conditions in which we live and develop were not always the same from the beginning.

The study of catastrophic events that took place in historical times, as late as the beginning of the seventh century before the present era, and on a greater scale eight hundred
years earlier, in the fifteenth century before the present era,
these being the last of a series of such events—a study
offered in *Worlds in Collision*—makes it abundantly clear
that more than once our planet escaped destruction by a
narrow margin. Further, in times past neither the size nor
the form of the Earth's orbit, nor the duration of its year and
its seasons, nor the direction of its axis, nor the rate of rotation and thus the length of the day, were the same as at present. Thus fate willed that the Earth should survive—but
whether it was by blind fate or by a protective Providence,
we are, as I put it at the end of *Earth in Upheaval*, "descendants of survivors, themselves descendants of survivors."

In such close brushes with a fatal destiny, not all species
left survivors—multitudes of forms of life were destroyed to
the last member. Especially abundant were total casualties
among mammals, and also among birds, amphibians and
fish.

The lesson learned from the history of the globe is that it
passed from one condition to another—changed position in
space, changed climate and order of seasons, with different
distribution of water and land—and that throughout the pre-
human and prehistoric periods there occurred even greater
cataclysms than exist in the memory of man, as the geological and paleontological records teach us. Yet some of the animal forms, like the tiny foraminifera in the ocean, succeeded
in surviving, at least in part, without going through complete
metamorphosis.

From the fact that in a matter of merely ten thousand
years man made the passage from the stage of unpolished
stone (Paleolithic) all the way to the so-called Western
civilization of our day—and ten thousand years is but about

one half of one millionth of the age of the Earth, as the modern geophysicists assess it—one must conclude that Nature, while destroying many, wished to create ever better conditions for at least some of those destined to survive as species.

Learning of the perilous path man and his animal companions traveled in eons past to reach conditions felicitous for procreation and advance, one cannot but wonder again whether Providence planned and willed it, or whether a blind fate was behind our survival, when so many forms of life were extinguished and when other planets fared so much less happily.

As it is now, man is the prince of Creation; Earth is the most fortunate planet in the solar system and the Sun's most important role is to care for us, inhabitants of Earth. If there were civilizations on any of the other planets, they are no more: there is only one civilization for the Sun to serve—the civilization of man.

Chapter I

OF RACIAL MEMORY

AN AMNESIA VICTIM

A victim of amnesia may live adjacent to neighbors who are completely unaware of his plight. He may be employed, he may be married, he may behave on the surface like anybody else. But he has forgotten everything before a certain date. He does not know his name and he assumes a new name to hide his own perplexity; he does not remember his childhood and adolescence or maturity prior to that date; he does not know the town or city from which he came and how he got to his new habitat; he does not know whether he was married formerly nor whether he has children. If he comes into conflict with the law, as for instance for bigamy, he may wind up in a psychiatric clinic; in most cases victims of amnesia voluntarily seek psychiatric help.

Amnesia need not erase all memory; it may affect only certain areas of the past. Such cases are very numerous and rarely is a neurotic personality free from some area of oblivion; characteristically, the oblivion erases the most painful or terrorizing reminiscences. Psychoanalysis, as Sigmund Freud conceived it, is a tool for bringing into the conscious mind the memories that have sunk into the subconscious stratum of the mind. This dredging up of a partial amnesia, if successful, is destined to heal the person of his irrational behavior: irrational or pathological reactions and pursuits are symptoms of a neurosis. In the early days, psychoanalysis was called katharsis by Freud, because by getting a sick person once again to live through a painful scene, Freud was able to restore the mental health of the patient and free him or her from pathological reactions. Freud's very first patient was a young lady who became the victim of a paralyzing neurosis, upon having submerged, as Freud found, the most painful memory of the circumstances of the death of her father whom she had nursed.

Another of the pathological forms to which an amnesia may lead is what is called mental scotoma. In ophthalmology, scotoma is a partial or insular blindness; a certain segment of the field of vision does not register on the retina because of some defect, like detachment of the retina or a clot of blood beneath it. Psychological scotoma is an inability to observe certain phenomena or to recognize certain situations though they are obvious to other persons. A man may not see an evident fact or not recognize an obvious situation, though his intelligence and rationality should produce an immediate realization and proper reaction. The proverbial husband of the promiscuous wife is the only one with no suspicion whatsoever; psychologically, most probably, the husband's unawareness of such a situation is conditioned by suppressed homosexuality producing a blindness to the state of affairs.

Whereas the phenomenon of total amnesia is rare, the observance of partial amnesia or psychological scotoma are daily experiences in psychiatry and psychoanalysis, and the reader himself most probably has "succeeded" in erasing from the conscious memory some painful occurrences, greater or smaller, that his ego cannot face. Much of maladjustment, failure and floundering, guilt feeling and self-punishment, or aggressiveness, hatred and hostility, pathological inclinations and sexual aberrations, criminal impulses and acts, suicide and murder, or detachment from reality and flight into madness can be traced by correctly applied analytical procedure to impressions erased from the conscious memory, traumatic occurrences obliterated—in short, to contents submerged. From the mind's dark recesses they pilot the personality toward its bizarre behavior and, not seldom, toward a repetition of the traumatic experience. This repetition is sought in the form of a return to the scene of the first experience, or in a fixation on abnormal sexual objects, or in selection of an occupation offering a regular substitute for an act repressed from the conscious memory.

In *Jenseits des Lustprinzips* (Beyond the Pleasure Principle), published in 1920, as also in several others of his works, Freud developed the thesis that "the patient cannot recollect everything he repressed—and quite possibly the most important part of it stays repressed. . . . He is, however, urged to repeat the repressed instead of recollecting it."

Freud spoke of this compulsion for repeating as of demoniac quality (*triebhafter, dämonischer Charakter*); the one possessed by it "lives in a dark anxiety (*dunkle Angst*), afraid of awakening something that would be better left asleep."

MIND'S FRONTIERS

The human mind is the least known territory, though through it man has obtained the entire sum of his experience and knowledge. Tests are made, IQs evaluated, psychological theories are written, psychotherapies are practiced, the action of drugs on the sensorium and behavior are studied, sex hormones are explored, the inner secretions of the pituitary gland are examined, brains are dissected, experiments on animals are made—and many discoveries are registered. But after all the efforts, some cardinal issues are as much in darkness now as they were thousands of years ago.

Are all the facilities of the brain subject to tests and evaluation? What is the thinking process? Does a person have a soul as well as a mind? Where is its seat? Certainly it is not in the heart, though common expression makes of the heart a seat of the emotions. A damage to a part of the brain as in arteriosclerosis or in a massive shock may lead to an irreparable loss of memory—does the soul thus perish, and does it die fully when the individual dies? Does the soul have communion with unknown forces; does it survive the body? Theology and spiritualism tear at the problem with little evidence and unproven results.

A probe touching a cell in the brain makes a forgotten memory vivid, so vivid that the person believes himself to be living in a situation that actually took place many years before.

We have seen a person susceptible to hypnosis receive an oral order to be unable to see or to hear or to move an arm— and comply with the order. Is this just a pretense on the subject's part? But the same person receives an order to be like a rigid rod and, upon being placed between two chairs, head on one and heels on the edge of the other, he or she—even a slight woman—in this cataleptic state can support the weight of several persons. Whence comes this physical reserve, unavailable in the conscious life, to the person now in catalepsy? And how can an oral order—nothing but sound— mobilize this reserve?

A person in hypnosis is given a suggestion to perform some act at a given time, possibly days after the hypnotic session, and to forget the command until time for its execution. Without being consciously aware of the suggestion and without a timepiece, the individual executes the command precisely on time. Is it, then, that a time-measuring device is implanted in the human brain? What causes forgetting and remembering?

Least of all does the hypnotist—be he a trained psychiatrist or an uneducated variety performer—know what makes hypnosis work. What are the physical and mental reserves that can be brought into action with the simplest of tools, a human word or gesture? The limits are suddenly so much wider that the capabilities used in daily life seem but one octave of a full keyboard.

At postdoctorate courses in medicine that I attended in the early twenties in Berlin we were given a chance to examine a ten-year-old mentally retarded boy who could, with almost the speed of a computer (then not yet in existence), tell the day in the week of any date, such as the birthdays of the participants in the course. If such capacity is present in one, what makes it unattainable in others?

Dervishes in an autohypnotic state walk on burning coals and suffer no ill effect; skin can be cut and blood ordered not to flow. A person in a trance can reportedly speak a language that he or she never learned or even heard. All this was known and practiced since very early times—"to speak with other tongues" as in Acts (2:4); to be made temporarily blind as in Genesis (19:11) and in the Second Book of Kings (6:18), *sanverim* in my understanding being the term for hypnosis in biblical Hebrew.

Extrasensory perception is a field explored and debated by the credulous and by the skeptical; sides are taken as if it were a matter of conviction and not of knowledge. The experiments at Duke University in North Carolina suffer from neglect of attention to the emotional state of the sender as well as of the recipient, as if such a state had no influence on the transmission of thoughts or messages from one individual to another. So much deception, voluntary or involuntary, has been introduced into the field of spiritualism, with materialization (ectoplasm), automatic writing, telekinesis, etc., that, though necromancy is at least as old as the story of the witch of En-Dor (I Samuel 28:7), nothing can be claimed with assurance for the credit or debit side of the ledger. This is true even though such a clear thinker as the physicist Oliver Lodge or such a wizard of detective invention as Arthur Conan Doyle sided with what must be termed the miraculous.

A feeling persists that though mental processes are physiological—and therefore in the last analysis physical and chemical—there are screens in man himself that hide from him a large part of the house he calls soul, this being the sum of all mind's activities, past and present, and all perception received or inherited, and that may or may not transcend the barriers of time, a metaphysical entity itself.

COLLECTIVE UNCONSCIOUS MIND

In 1930 I spent the summer on a "working vacation" in Zürich. During the preceding winter I had written a paper "On the Physical Existence of the World of Thought." In Küssnacht, near Zürich, I visited Professor Eugen Bleuler, for decades the undisputed dean of psychiatry. It was Bleuler who opened the doors of academia to Sigmund Freud by assigning his (Bleuler's) assistant Carl Jung at Burghölzli mental hospital to study Freudian theory with a view to its application in the wards. Bleuler and Freud both were born in 1856, but while Freud was a "loner," rejected and hardly ever mentioned in medical periodicals unless in disrepute, Bleuler dominated the field.

In that paper of mine I dealt with certain problems near the borderline of the then legitimate psychiatry: I claimed that physical processes underlie mental processes; I maintained that it should be possible to make the blind see and the deaf hear by reaching the brain centers with adequate electrical impulses, thus circumventing the peripheral sensorial organs. I postulated engrams in brain cells as carriers of memory—and, it followed, the engrams could be reawakened by suitable mechanical impulses. I maintained that encephalograms of persons suffering from epilepsy would show a disorderly and violent wave pattern as if caused by short circuits: until then only one paper on the encephalogram in men—and that in healthy men—had been published, by Hans Berger of Jena.[1] I wrote:

At an excitation of a peripheral sense organ, for instance, an eye by a strong light, there appears a current oscillation in the opposite optical region. . . . I think it would be worthwhile to apply the experiments of Berger on epileptics. The lightning start of an epileptic seizure reminds me strongly of the action of a short circuit. . . . Then it would be proper also to experiment with the possibility of relieving the too strong oscillations (*Stromschwankungen*) of the current in the brain of the epileptics. This should be regarded as a preliminary communication.

I also claimed the existence of a collective mind in the early stages of the development of the species. Individualization accompanies the evolution from lower to higher forms, yet the collective mind is never fully erased in man; it comes to the fore preferably in excited states of mind, also in crowds swept by emotions. On this score I wrote:

It transpires ever clearer that the autonomy of the mental domains of separate individuals must have developed as a more complicated and higher state in the origin of the species. In our concept telepathy is an archaic form of thought-transmission. The more a species is developed, the more is

[1] *"Elektrencephalogramm des Menschen,"* Archiv für Psychiatrie und Nervenkrankheiten (1929), pp. 527 ff.

the single creature separated as a thinking ego from the world around it.

The migration of the young birds that fly toward the homeland of their parents, the collective work of ants and bees, which understand how to execute a great work following a common plan, and similar examples speak for a not too sharp division of the mental life of one animal from that of the others. . . . This archaic form of reciprocal influence shows itself in the animal herd and also in the human herd, the mass.

Bleuler discussed my paper with me and willingly acceded to my desire that he should write an introduction to it. In his introduction Bleuler said:

Out of a mass of superstition, illusion and deceit, facts were retrieved for which the so-called natural explanations failed completely; these facts are numerous enough to compel science to make them the object of a very careful study. Therefore, an attempt to bring them into correlation with known natural laws is very useful; it can not only stimulate scientific thought, but also help to overcome the fear—incompatible with science—of entering a new and very unusual domain.

The ideas of the author appear to me very much worthy of consideration. I myself came upon very similar, in essential aspects quite identical concepts, even if I cannot subscribe to every detail. If the work [of Dr. V.] contributes only so much that one would be able to speak about these matters without being thought crazy or, at the least, inferior—it already serves science, independently of how much of its content will stand future research.

Upon my return to Mt. Carmel, near Haifa, where I then lived and practiced, I sent the paper to Europe for publication in some journal dedicated to psychiatric research. After one rejection, the name of Bleuler prevailed and the prestigious *Zeitschrift für die gesammte Neurologie und Psychiatrie* published it in 1931.[2] I sent a copy of the printed article to Freud, who answered, as usual, in longhand. His letter reads:

Dear Colleague: 24th June, 1931

I find myself in complete agreement with Bleuler on the contents of your paper (*Energetik der Psyche*). I, too, have independently formed my own opinions on the subject which come very close to yours and which in some parts quite coincide with them. It is exactly the analyst who has the least objection to an energetic interpretation of the processes of thought. My own experiences have led me to suppose that telepathy is the real core of the alleged parapsychological phenomena and maybe the only one. But in these matters I have neither experienced anything compelling nor have I found it anywhere else—not even in your paper.[3] Therefore, nothing remains to us but to await clarification of this basically physical problem from the hopefully not too distant future.

> With friendly greetings
> your
> Freud

The understanding of the collective unconscious mind may explain many phenomena observed in social animals, like ants and bees, working on a common plan. Anybody who has observed the behavior of large shoals of fish, numbering in the thousands, changing instantaneously and si-

---

[2] *"Ueber die Energetik der Psyche und die physikalische Existenz der Gedankenwelt. Ein Beitrag zur Psychologie des gesunden und somnambulen Zustandes," Zeitschrift für die gesammte Neurologie und Psychiatrie,* 133 (1931), pp. 422–37.

[3] It was not the purpose of my paper to present extensive case materials. Cf. my paper "Very Similar, Almost Identical" in *Psychoanalysis and the Future: A Centenary Commemoration of the Birth of Sigmund Freud* (New York, 1957), pp. 14–17, 152–53.

multaneously the direction of their swim, finds it difficult to explain the simultaneity of action as mimicry; it appears more plausible that the fish act as they do by impulses of a common mind—the collective mind of a crowd, all members of which are reacting identically to a given impulse.

The question then arises whether a collective mind is a product merely of some process akin to telepathy, or whether it may also link consecutive generations. This is a highly important problem bearing on nothing less than the ultimate fate of the human race, and with it, on the rest of the population of the planet.

JUNG'S ARCHETYPES

After ten years of Freud's "splendid isolation" (1895–1905), a circle of disciples gathered around him; not many years later several of them, notably Wilhelm Stekel, Alfred Adler and Carl Jung, built their own theories and schools and also claimed success in therapy. Whereas Adler stressed the sociological aspects and the urge for recognition and the will for power as the mainsprings of behavior, Jung indulged in mythical subjects and searched the world literature on alchemy, the cabala, and the dreams of mystics to find a pathway of his own. In the study of the unconscious he started as Freud's disciple, but after the schism he denied his debt. In 1916, soon after parting with the master, he came up with an early version of the concept of racial memory; in this he might have been, though he would not admit it, elaborating on some ideas Freud offered in *Totem and Tabu* (1912). In that work Freud maintained that quite a few reactions in family situations reflect some racial unconscious vestiges of acts, among them patricide, committed by the cave man of the Stone Age.

In the summer of 1930 I visited Jung in his house near

Zürich and, unaware of the degree of his antagonism toward Freud, I referred to him as Freud's disciple, to which he strongly objected.

In 1934 Jung came up with the idea of the collective unconscious mind, and in the following years he developed this concept. He wrote in his *Archetypes of the Collective Unconscious* (1934):

"At first the concept of the unconscious was limited to denoting the state of repressed or forgotten contents. Even with Freud . . . it is really nothing but the gathering place of forgotten and repressed contents. . . . For Freud, accordingly, the unconscious is of an exclusively personal nature, although he was aware of its archaic and mythological thought-forms."

In a footnote, Jung conceded that Freud "in his later works" differentiated between "the instinctual psyche" of a human being, called by him the "id," and his "super-ego," which "denotes the collective consciousness, of which the individual is partly conscious and partly unconscious (because it is repressed)."

Jung continued: "A more or less superficial layer of the unconscious is undoubtedly personal. I call it the *personal unconscious*. But this personal unconscious rests upon a deeper layer, which does not derive from personal experience and is not a personal acquisition but is inborn. This deeper layer I call the *collective unconscious*. I have chosen the term 'collective' because this part of the unconscious is not individual but universal; in contrast to the personal psyche, it has contents and modes of behavior that are more or less the same everywhere and in all individuals. It is, in other words, identical in all men and thus constitutes a common psychic substrate of a suprapersonal nature which is present in every one of us."

The contents of the personal unconscious are, according to Jung, "feeling-toned complexes"; the contents of the collective unconscious are "archetypes." This term is met already in the first century Alexandrian philosopher Philo Judaeus, who thus called the God image in man. With Jung, "archetypes" are archaic or primordial—they are "images that have existed since the remotest times." But in myth, in "esoteric teaching," in dreams and visions and fairy tales, they manifest themselves: "The archetype is essentially an unconscious content that is altered by becoming conscious and being perceived."

Jung realized that in myth an "unconscious psychic process" is at work and therefore futile is the work of mythologists who have "always helped themselves out with solar, lunar, meteorological, vegetal, and other ideas of the kind" and "absolutely refused" to see that the mythological images and contents reflect deep, ingrained psychic phenomena. And "what is true of primitive lore is true in even higher degree of the ruling world religions. They contain a revealed knowledge that was originally hidden." (I would have said "a hidden knowledge that was originally revealed.")

Symbols employed in the religions are representations of hidden contents. "Dogma takes the place of the collective unconscious by formulating its contents on a grand scale"; but "the Catholic way of life is completely unaware of psychological problems in this sense. Almost the entire life of the collective unconscious has been channeled into the dogmatic archetypal ideas and flows along like a well-controlled stream in the symbolism of creed and ritual. . . . Before the Christian Church existed there were the antique mysteries, and these reach back into the gray mists of neolithic prehistory." The Church created a protective wall of sacred images. "People had long since forgotten what they meant. Or had they really forgotten? Could it be that men had never really known what they meant? . . . actually we haven't the remotest conception of what is meant by the Virgin Birth, the divinity of Christ, and the complexities of the Trinity. . . . The fact is that archetypal images are so packed with meaning in themselves that people never think of asking what they really do mean. . . . And when [a person] starts thinking about them, he does so with the help of what he calls 'reason'—which in point of fact is nothing more than the sum-total of all his prejudices and myopic views."[4]

I tried to extract from Jung a clear line of thought. Actually, however, he is hardly able to pursue one theme; in his writing he follows the flight of thoughts or "free associations," diverting all the time on tangents. He speaks of the *chronique scandaleuse* of Olympus, of the disintegration of Protestantism "into nearly four hundred denominations," of "the alarming poverty of symbols" in them, and of the void that yawns before the modern man in need of symbols. Jung himself winds up with a yearning for Oriental religions, containing an unfathomed wisdom and symbolism not understood, "the allurements of the odorous East," the esoteric teachings; and he professes an absorbing curiosity in, and almost an identification with, certain mystics and hermits of the past centuries. The readers, however, wish to know more of the archetypes and, if it should follow, how to apply the teaching to the treatment of single persons, or if possible of the human race. Drifting clouds make an opening and we read:

> Mankind is powerless against mankind, and the gods, as ever, show it the ways of fate. . . . In the realm of consciousness we are our own masters. . . . But if we step through the door of the shadow we discover with terror that we are the objects of unseen factors. To know this is decidedly unpleasant, for nothing is more disillusioning than the discovery of our own inadequacy. It can even give rise to

[4] Carl G. Jung, *The Archetypes and the Collective Unconscious*, translated by R.F.C. Hull (Princeton University Press, 1968), pp. 3–7, 12–13.

primitive panic, because, instead of being believed in, the anxiously guarded supremacy of consciousness—which is in truth one of the secrets of human success—is questioned in the most dangerous way. But since ignorance is no guarantee of security, and in fact only makes our insecurity still worse, it is probably better despite our fear to know where the danger lies.

Jung asked the question, and let it follow by intuitively felt concern though not by an answer:

To ask the right question is already half the solution of a problem. At any rate we then know that the greatest danger threatening us comes from the unpredictability of the psyche's reactions. Discerning persons have realized for some time that external historical conditions, of whatever kind, are only occasions, jumping-off grounds, for the real dangers that threaten our lives. These are the present politico-social delusional systems. We should not regard them casually, as necessary consequences of external conditions, but as decisions precipitated by the collective unconscious.[5]

It seems that Jung had world communism in mind; for national-socialism's upsurge, as some scholars have brought to light, Jung had only an attitude of sympathy and did not describe it as a delusional system; with Judeo-Christianity he felt an urge to part. The gods of Valhalla were closer to him than the God of Sinai or that of Golgotha. As a Verrazano who saw a stream and failed to penetrate it, but registered his discovery, Jung formulated his concept:

My thesis, then, is as follows: In addition to our immediate consciousness, which is of a thoroughly personal nature and which we believe to be the only empirical psyche (even

[5] Ibid., pp. 13–15, 23.

if we tack on the personal unconscious as an appendix), there exists a second psychic system of a collective, universal, and impersonal nature which is identical in all individuals. This collective unconscious does not develop individually, but is inherited. It consists of pre-existent forms, the archetypes. . . .[6]

"Pre-existent" means since the emergence of the human race. What made these forms populate man's mind was never explained by Jung. He did not attempt to approach the phenomenon by a study of animal instincts. In many analytical situations he saw an archetype. Thus a recurrent motif of having had two mothers was explained as an archetype (a simpler explanation would be in the binding ties to a mother and a wet-nurse). Ever increasing the number of archetypes by adding all kinds of recurring concepts, some of questionable nature, Jung moved the psychoanalytical endeavor of his group to a recognition of archetypes in patients' dreams and fantasies, also in behavior, and thus encouraged his followers to ever greater application of the concept of archetypes to trivial fantasies or patterns of behavior.

The sublime question, almost the awful quest—How did some true archetypes enter the human mind and settle there to plague it, and to pass from generation to generation?—was not even asked.

FREUD'S DESCENT INTO HADES

By 1913 Freud had parted with Jung, who tended to mysticism, and with Adler, who tended to socialism. In that year Freud published *Totem and Tabu*, an analytical study of ancient and partly also of modern folklore culled mostly from Frazer's *Golden Bough*. Freud endeavored to evince from

[6] Ibid., p. 43.

various rites and observances the surviving traces of patricide practices in the cave of prehistoric man: the grown-
up sons used to kill their fathers and possess their mothers, a
violent act in consummation of the Oedipus complex, the
son's sexual attachment to his mother. Freud "felt that religious ceremonials and individual psychological reactions
still bear witness to the unconscious persistence of memories
of archaic situations, anxieties, feelings of guilt, and various
reaction formations which are beyond contemporary experience."[7]

Freud came to this understanding rather late in his analytical work. For almost a score of years he ascribed the origin of neuroses exclusively to the traumatic experiences in
the early life of a person, usually in his second to fifth years.

Freud moved slowly toward the new orientation. What he
used to call the unconscious was the personal unconscious
or, if we prefer, the subconscious; in deeper recesses of the
mind were stored racial memories; instincts, too, belong to
the racial heritage.

The longer Freud sat behind the couch and the more he
listened and thought, the more the concept of guilt feeling
for acts committed by ancestors grew in persuasiveness. Archetypes inborn in primogenitors of man were foreign to
Freud: ancestral man *acquired* the guilt feeling when he
committed the act of patricide. Further, he committed his
issue, not seldom an incestuous progeny, to *repeat* his own
act and to will to later generations the urge again to repeat
and suffer guilt—or at least to imitate in an unconscious urge
and still suffer guilt. A traumatic experience in an individual
asks to be repeated; to the traumatic experiences of his ancestors he is an heir. Freud knew of no other paramount
trauma that could become a source of universal guilt feeling.

In "From the History of an Infantile Neurosis" (1918),
Freud explained the universality of certain symbolic expres-

---

[7] "Racial Memory," *Encyclopedia of Psychoanalysis* (1968), p. 361.

sions in speech and in various fantasies, usually connected with parental coitus and the related castration fears, as grounded in persisting unconscious memories of archaic situations.

> We must finally make up our minds to adopt the hypothesis that the psychical precipitates of the primeval period became inherited property which, in each fresh generation, called not for acquisition but only for awakening. . . . We find that in a number of important relations our children react, not in a manner corresponding to their own experience, but instinctively, like the animals, in a manner that is only explicable as phylogenetic acquisition.[8]

A neurotic state results from triggering an explosive precipitate inherited from ancestral generations.

> Early trauma–defence–latency–outbreak of neurotic illness–partial return of the repressed. Such is the formula which we have laid down for the development of a neurosis. The reader is now invited to take the step of supposing that something occurred in the life of the human species similar to what occurs in the life of individuals: of supposing, that is, that here too events occurred of a sexually aggressive nature, which left behind them permanent consequences but were for the most part fended off and forgotten, and which after a long latency came into effect and created phenomena similar to symptoms in their structure and purpose.[9]

Here Freud assigned equal roles to the personal and to the inherited trauma:

> As a rule there is a combination of both factors, the constitutional and the accidental. The stronger the consti-

---

[8] Freud, *Moses and Monotheism* in *Works*, edited by James Strachey (1955), vol. 23, pp. 132–33.

[9] Ibid., p. 80.

tutional factor, the more readily will a trauma lead to a fixation and leave behind a developmental disturbance; the
stronger the trauma, the more certainly will its injurious
effects become manifest even when the instinctual situation
is normal.[10]

But can the "instinctual situation" be normal if everyone
in the human race is a carrier of traumatic experience of
earlier generations? Freud is not yet clear. Averse to use any
Jungian terms or concepts, he delineated as "id" the unconscious domain of a person, a repository of the phylogenetic
and instinctual heritage and equally so of personal experiences and reactions repressed and forgotten due to their
traumatic character.

> It [the id] contains everything that is inherited, that is
> present at birth, that is laid down in the constitution—above
> all, therefore, the instincts, which originate from the somatic
> organization and which find a first psychical expression here
> [in the id] in forms unknown to us.[11]

This passage was inserted by Freud in 1938 into his *Outline of Psychoanalysis*. Likewise the following passage was
included by him as the result of his analytical experience between 1913 and 1938:

> Some portion of the cultural acquisitions have undoubt-
> edly left a precipitate behind them in the id; much of what
> is contributed by the super-ego will awaken an echo in the
> id; not a few of the child's new experiences will be in-

[10] Freud, "Analysis Terminable and Interminable," in *Works*, edited by
Strachey, vol. 23, p. 220.
[11] Freud, *An Outline of Psychoanalysis*, Part 1, ch. 1, in *Works*, edited
by Strachey, vol. 23, p. 145.

tensified because they are repetitions of some primeval phylogenetic experience.[12]

Since many instinctual reactions and arrangements serve the species and even enable it to survive, a demarcation line needs to be drawn between the heritage of instincts of beneficial purpose and the deeply imbedded phylogenetic memories of violent traumas. Likewise, Oedipal attachment and parricide do not belong in the same group with instincts serving survival. Nor do the personal traumas repressed into oblivion belong in the same category or come to be stored in the same layer of the unconscious as "something that occurred in the life of the human species," as Freud put it, "of a sexually aggressive nature."

These are some of the most important postulates of the psychoanalytic theory as formulated by Sigmund Freud—they concern the traumatic experiences, their frequent suppression and removal from the conscious memory, the urge to relive them and by doing so to inflict a similar trauma on somebody else, thus reversing the roles.

Freud says in *Jenseits des Lustprinzips* (Beyond the Pleasure Principle):

> At the outset he [the child] was in a *passive* situation—he was overpowered by the experience; but by repeating it, unpleasurable though it was, as a game, he took on an *active* part. . . . As the child passes over from the passivity of the experience to the activity of the game, he hands on the disagreeable experience to one of his playmates and in this way revenges himself on a substitute.[13]

In the traumatic experience terror and anguish play the decisive role. Sometimes the memory of the traumatic expe-

---

[12] Ibid., pp. 206–7.

[13] Freud, *Beyond the Pleasure Principle*, sect. II, pp. 16–17, in *Works*, edited by Strachey, vol. XVIII.

rience is not forgotten and yet the urge to relive it may persist; but the urge to relive is definitely greater when the experience itself is repressed and relegated to the subconscious mind. The victim of amnesia caused by a traumatic experience lives under the urge to repeat the experience, often reversing the roles, himself becoming the aggressor and inflicting punishment on a new victim.

OF RACIAL MEMORY

Whether acquired characteristics are inheritable is a question that has generated scientific debate and inquiry since the days of Lamarck. He was a proponent of such inheritance and it is usually asserted that Darwin, two generations later, was its opponent. The truth is that Darwin in his theory of gemmules (1868) subscribed to the view that each cell in an organism sends its imprint to the reproduction cells (germs or plasma) and that this is how inheritance of parental features takes place; in such an arrangement acquired characteristics would naturally be hereditary. New characteristics of wheat or rye cultivated in a changed environment could become inherited: a rugged stem could develop, for instance, when a plant grew year after year in latitudes of short summers, windy falls, and late springs. How long such inheritance would persist if the plant were repatriated to its earlier soil and climate, is at the base of the modern dispute about the inheritance of acquired characteristics.

A change in the germ cells (sperm, ova) would result in inheritable new characteristics; but it is assumed that only somatic cells are susceptible to variation. Yet it cannot be denied that chemical processes or endocrine disturbances in an organism can decidedly influence the plasma cells, in which case the progeny would exhibit an inherited defect which occasionally can also be transmitted to subsequent generations.

The question thus boils down to the problem of whether outside influences—via the somatic cells or even directly—can affect the germ cells. Somatic cells—which make up the body of a living organism—live their span of time, and return to the metabolic process of nature, or to dust. The germ cells, however, carry life for untold generations, using the individual organism as their carrier. These cells are potentially immortal, though an enormous proportion of them goes to waste as anyone can witness who sees the seeds of trees or pollen lost, or thinks of the billions of spermatozoa ejected in a single copulation with usually only one of this multitude having a chance of fertilization. Remarkable is the endless reproduction capability stored in a single microscopic sperm or egg, with inheritable characteristics for generations without end. And it is not that a spermatozoon is inherited and multiplies again, but that the new organism has reproductive cells which produce the new sperm and egg. If these reproductive cells, or the sperm and egg, are influenced by some strong chemical, thermal or radioactive agent, the new characteristics may well become inheritable —and this opens the way to enormous possibilities in genetics.

Paroxysms in nature, accompanied by such agents, could influence the reproductive cells of the animal and plant kingdoms; if, as happened more than once, the area involved in a paroxysm were the entire world, then chances would be excellent for mutations to occur in many species and genera. The germ cells could be affected not only through the soma, or body, but also directly, with the subsequent origin and transmission of new characteristics. And since the same causes could conceivably result in similar changes, especially in forms that procreate with more than one offspring at a time, perpetuation of new forms, if only viable for life, would result.

The question whether strong impressions made on an animal's sensorium are the basis of instincts is a problem that requires more deliberation than space here permits—and also some ingenious experimentation. The existence of a racial memory does not mean that an impression absorbed by one generation can be remembered by the following ones, but that impressions, especially traumatic and repetitious impressions, experienced by many of the forebears, may become a permanent though unconscious mneme or mneme complex, providing adequate responses in suitable situations.

A racial memory is not a transmigration of the soul; it is, however, an inherited unconscious memory. And through a racial memory we can consider ourselves as having been present at some horrible cataclysmic scenes amid unchained elements, devastation by which no creature in the world, on land or in the sea, could conceivably have been unaffected. Thus the accumulation of the genetic mnemes comes down to every representative of the species in our days through every one of the genealogical lines: all ascendancy reaches back to the same generation that was exposed to the trauma.

At approaching earthquakes, animals with fine sensoria flee, before seismographs even register any tremor. During forest fires, animals that normally live in terror of other animals will run together with their predators, struck by a greater terror, to cave shelters.

It is quite obvious that some information—called instinct—is being reawakened and reactivated, with fear never absent.

The racial memory of a species is a matter of fact: it tells a wild creature how to build its nest, how to provide food, how to find a mate for procreation, how to survive in open spaces or in a long winter; but the most devastating experiences are also the most deeply buried and their reawakening is accompanied by a sensation of terror.

MANKIND'S DELUSION

The octogenarian founder of psychoanalysis was not yet at the end of his insights and revelations. A repressed thought was asking to be spelled out.

If we consider mankind as a whole and substitute it for a single individual, we discover that it too has developed delusions which are inaccessible to logical criticism and which contradict reality. If, in spite of this, they [the delusions] are able to exert an extraordinary power over men, investigation leads us to the same explanation as in the case of the single individual. They owe their power to the element of *historical truth* which they have brought up from the repression of the forgotten and primeval past.[14] [Italics in text.]

Freud speaks here of mankind's delusions, therefore delusions in which all of us take part and which are deaf to logical criticism; at the bottom, however, is a historical truth.

What, then, is this truth, the happening that once overwhelmed the human race and traumatized and poisoned and scorched the minds of all generations that followed? Was it a bedtime story? Was it a nursery discovery of every infant? And did this drama happen as regularly as Freud thought it did? Was the natural process of reproduction, though not all trauma-free, devised as all aberration? Is the

---

[14] Freud, "Construction in Analysis," in *Works*, edited by Strachey, vol. 23, p. 269.

ubiquitous murder of the father by the son *the* "historical
truth"? And if so, which historical truth would resuscitate
neurosis in the female? Or are males alone affected by the
delusions of the human race?

Freud lacked the final insight. During the years when a
scourge by the most evil of men caused hearts to throb with
fear and faces to pale, the Jew Freud, in once happy Vienna,
now for five long years (1933–38) doomed any day to see
Hakenkreutz banners on the streets and storm troopers
banging on the door, was called by his "id" and by his
"superego" alike to listen to a hardly audible voice from a
greater depth. In nights of anguish, with his cancerous jaw
paining, deserted even by his patients,* he was closer than
ever to the "historical truth," at least by sensing that he had
not yet discovered it as he earlier had thought.

We followed Freud in his early observations that a traumatic experience of psychic or physical nature often results
in amnesia. We further followed Freud in his realization
that a victim of amnesia either denies the trauma or makes
an effort to relive it.

When Freud, in a later and deeper penetration into the
human soul, discerned the buried racial memories of traumatic experiences of our progenitors, we followed Freud,
now with bated breath, once more. But we knew this time he
would fail. The great human trauma was not what he imag-
ined it to be—the killing of the father and the possession of
the mother by the grown sons now capable of overpowering
the father, the tyrant in the cave. And symptomatically, following his own diagnosis of behavior, Freud returned in his
last book to the days of the Exodus, only to display a scotoma—no plagues, no convulsion of nature, no terrifying ex-

---

* From a letter by Freud to A. Zweig.

periences at Mount Sinai, only the stoning of Moses, the father symbol, by the children of Israel in the desert.[15]

Freud was nearly correct in his diagnosis when he wrote that mankind lives in a state of delusion, but he was unable to define the etiology: in this case, the nature of the traumatic experience.

In the frame of collective amnesia, which is the syndrome I first discussed in *Worlds in Collision,* the amnesia that occurs in a single victim closely following the trauma is not an exact parallel: the collective mind does not immediately forget what it went through. What occupies us are the two processes in which the heritage was transmitted: the conscious oral and later written relay, and the unconscious, racial mneme, inherited and occasionally activated after some related experiences.

Psychoanalysis as it is practiced today ignores Freud's deeper insights. But, loath to read the testimony of the witnesses of celestial and terrestrial order turned to chaos—a terror chilling the very marrow of the bones—psychoanalysis was prudent not to follow Freud and stopped a great step earlier, not recognizing the importance of the role of biological inheritance of acquired characteristics in mental spheres on a collective basis. Yet, many new possibilities would open up, and numerous of the observed expressions of neurosis would be understood, with some knowledge of what happened to humanity in ages past.

THE ARCHAIC TRAUMA

Quite a few phenomena of both neuroses of fear and neuroses of compulsion, though they may have been triggered by early infantile experiences, have their roots in ar

[15] Freud, *Der Mann Moses und die monotheistische Religion* (Amsterdam, 1939).

chaic situations. They are of the nature of reactions to life-threatening circumstances. Individuals who are afraid of closed spaces, or panicked by wide-open areas, or fear views from heights, or flight in planes, may perchance be exhibiting atavistic fears engendered in the catastrophic experiences of ancestors. And as in structural biology in which a derivation of six fingers may often be traced to the same deformity in a quite removed ancestor, and again to an earlier occurrence in farther removed progenitors, so also a psychic anomaly may possibly skip several generations, only to reappear as if in random cases.

One of the most traumatic collective experiences of mankind took place when the closely approaching foreign body caused the displacement of Earth's strata, producing agonizing shrieks. The early Greek poet and cosmologist Hesiod wrote of the inscrutable noise: "The huge earth groaned; the earth resounded terribly, and the wide heaven above."[16]

The people's agony was increased by the sensation of hardly being attached to the ground; the presence of the foreign body, and possibly some attending electrical effect, produced a sensation of near-weightlessness. Could it not be that the people who are afraid of rising from the ground in airplanes are victims of reawakened atavistic memories? People who are inordinately afraid of thunder, or afraid even to wet their feet in the sea, and others with incongruent neuroses of fear may also have their anamnesis from centuries or millennia before their birth. And, likewise, among the neuroses of compulsion there must be many instances traceable to racial traumas.

The reader should not draw the erroneous conclusion that the human psyche is nothing but a carrier of impressions en-

[16] *Theogony*, translated by H. Evelyn-White (Loeb Classical Library, 1914). 11. 820 ff., 852 ff.

gendered in catastrophic circumstances. Certainly such natural urges as satisfaction of thirst and hunger, sexual activity, parental—especially motherly—protection of offspring, the need for self-expression or self-assertion and recognition, social congregation, preoccupation with accumulation of material goods, and other drives, are all inborn in man—and hardly any of them is unknown in animal species, domesticated or wild. All these instincts are present in human beings, and without some of them life itself could not persist. But upheavals in nature, with the unleashing of frenzied elements, shocked the minds of survivors and left there an indelible, heritable impression.

Chapter II

TO KNOW AND NOT TO KNOW

I was compelled by logic and by evidence to penetrate
into so many premises of the house of science. I freely
admit to having repeatedly caused fires, though the can-
dle in my hand was carried only for illumination.

A RECONSTRUCTION OF EVENTS

The repeated destructions of the world, which happened
as far back as the recollection of man can reach, and especially the last destructions, impressed themselves on the
memories of various peoples around the world in a manner
not to be wiped away.

In my published books I offered a reconstruction of some
of these events from the historical past, a reconstruction
built upon studying the human testimony as preserved in
the heritage of all ancient civilizations. All of them, in texts
bequeathed from the time man learned to write, tell in various forms the narrative that the trained eye of a psychoanalyst could not but recognize as so many variants of the
same theme; in hymns, in prayers, in historical texts, in philosophical discourses, in records of astronomical observations, but also in legend and religious myth, the ancients

desperately tried to convey to their descendants, ourselves included, the record of events that left a strong imprint on the witnesses.

I told the story in a brutal manner, in the sense that there was little consideration for the complete unawareness of the readers, living with nearly absolute repression of the most significant of all racial memories, in almost complete oblivion of the tribulations that agitated their forebears.

In my analytical practice I would never have perplexed a patient with sudden revelation of the hidden motifs underlying an affliction, without a preceding lengthy preparation in which I would carefully guide the patient to his or her own insight. Only after such preliminary work had been done could a startling revelation be risked and even then, in some cases, the effect might be almost shattering—but by that time the avenues of retreat into ignorance would have already been blocked; by that time also the patient would have understood the good intentions of the analyst and a link of transference would have been forged. But in offering an anamnesis, or the story of the development of the repression, to a collective suffering from amnesia, I have not followed the same procedure—and I could not. Should I have told first a curtailed story of great upheavals of the past—a watered-down version—or administered it in small doses, a teaspoon after breakfast? Should I have presented the story as only possibly but not necessarily true? Should I have offered it as science fiction? Should I have printed it seriatim or dismembered it among obscure magazines?

I did as I did, realizing that a strong reaction would be generated in everyone who would come into contact with the disclosure, whether directly or through hearsay. In some, the reaction would take the form of vociferous denial, protest, accusation and the organization of opposition. In others—overwhelmed by a revelation—there would be an equally strong reaction of acceptance, acclamation and a rush of missionary zeal to convert others. The demarcation line that divided the camps ran with hardly any deviation between those who did not read the message published as *Worlds in Collision,* in 1950, and those who did. Those who did not read it had, nevertheless, very outspoken views; they knew "everything" by way of reviews, debates and gossip, while a spontaneous reaction forbade their reading the book itself.

The story told in that book is no mere hypothesis and no idle theory: it is a reconstruction of events that took place in the historical past, thirty-four and twenty-seven centuries ago, or, in the main, close to one hundred generations ago.

Each page of the text bears references to sources, and therefore the evidence presented is subject to control. The narrative is horrifying and doubly so. On the one hand is the anguished, bloodcurdling spectacle of our forebears suffering the paroxysms of nature. On the other hand is the horrifying realization that we were brought up in a deception—in a view of the past which is but a guile that dulled our inquiry, put our vibrant curiosity to sleep, taught us, together with our statesmen, philosophers and scientists, a lesson of apathy as to our true destinies, and at the same time imbued us with the self-assurance that nothing earth-shaking can happen to us.

But our planet *was* involved in traffic accidents. The length of the year, of the month and of the day have not remained unchanged since the beginning: they changed repeatedly in historical times when man was already perfectly literate and could leave records of the changes in writing. They are in various scripts, notably in the cuneiform. The data in cuneiform can be compared with the data in hieroglyphics, and both together can be compared with ancient calendars around the world, and with the sundials and water clocks of bygone days, now defunct not because of faulty construction, but because of changes in what they were designed to measure. These data can and should be examined in the light of historical records, and then should be investigated with respect to the meaning of sacred texts of every ancient religion, texts abundant in passages dealing with cosmic upheavals and with the legendary treasure of antiquity.

The literary record puts a clear picture before our eyes. Then we investigate the fields of natural history: if events of such a magnitude have taken place, there must be unequivocal evidence on land and at the bottom of the sea. A perusal of my *Earth in Upheaval* will convince even the most skeptical of readers that indeed no place on earth is free from this compelling evidence. In arctic regions in the past, coal was formed and corals grew; rhinoceroses, mammoths and buffalo left their bones in enormous profusion deep in the polar circle. In Africa, in China, in Brazil, in northern Europe and elsewhere, are animal conglomerates from tropical and polar regions—polar bears, arctic foxes, tropical snakes and crocodiles. Brown coal (lignite) is found to contain insect forms and plants thrown together from regions as far apart as Norway, Madagascar and Brazil. Mountain ridges rose to their present height in the age of man, even well-advanced man, and every exploring team returning from one of these major mountain chains—the Himalayas, the Caucasus, the Alps, the Andes—reported with astonishment this discovery of extreme recentness.

As I said, the story was brutally told and there could only be a strong reaction expected from such an analytical blunder, and indeed there was.

Yet, the liberating value of overcoming a repression of racial memories is much greater than the chance of psychological harm. The remedy lies in starting to teach my historical reconstruction in the schools, actually in the early grades. Thus there would be no conflict with views deeply rooted in the school textbooks of today; the process of reacquisition of the memories of ancient traumatic events will be much smoother and the shock, if any, will be thoroughly beneficial. These facts of life need to be communicated early in order to free them of the element of "secondary shock," the primary shock having been experienced by our ancestors in paroxysmal circumstances.

TO KNOW AND NOT TO KNOW

Freud wrote of two psychological reactions to a trauma. "The effects of the trauma are twofold, positive and negative. The former are endeavors to revive the trauma, to remember the forgotten experience, or, better still, to make it real—to live once more through a repetition of it. . . . These endeavors are summed up in the terms 'fixation to the trauma' and 'repetition compulsion.'" About the other reaction Freud wrote: "The negative reactions pursue the oppo site aim; here nothing is to be remembered or repeated of the forgotten traumata. They [the negative reactions] may be grouped together as defensive reactions. They express themselves in avoiding issues, a tendency which may culminate in an inhibition or phobia. These negative reactions also contribute considerably to the formation of character. Actually, they represent fixations on the trauma no less than do the positive reactions, but they follow the opposite tendency. The symptoms of the neurosis proper constitute a compromise, to which both the positive and negative effects of the trauma contribute; sometimes one component, sometimes the other, predominates. These opposite reactions create conflicts which the subject cannot as a rule resolve."[1]

[1] Freud, *Moses and Monotheism*, translated by K. Jones (New York, 1967), pp. 94–95.

ISAIAH

In literature from classical times and the early Christian centuries, and also later, we may observe a process whereby the events that occurred in earlier ages fell into oblivion. First there were those who knew—who witnessed the events and described what they saw.

The prophet Isaiah began to deliver his message in −747, in the days of King Uzziah, in the very day of the devastation caused by nature; he continued his orations as he grew into a statesman, addressing himself to the nation and its conscience, to the individual and his soul. As a master of the written word, Isaiah has no equal in world literature. No translation even remotely does justice to Isaiah's Hebrew—in its conciseness, its forcefulness, its richness of word and structure. Isaiah lived in the time of the last series of catastrophes, and he could not have described them more clearly:

Behold, the Lord maketh the earth empty, and maketh it waste, and turneth it upside down. . . . the inhabitants of the earth are burned, and few men [are] left.[2]

Fear, and the pit, and the snare are upon thee, O inhabitant of the earth. . . . for the windows from on high are open, and the foundations of the earth do shake. The earth is utterly broken down, the earth is clean dissolved, the earth is moved exceedingly.[3]

Isaiah describes it all—the changes in the sky, the upheavals on earth and sea, the quaking of mountains, the people fleeing, the migrations of entire nations.

The book of Isaiah, together with the writings of other

[2] Isaiah 24:1, 6.
[3] Isaiah 24:17–19.

prophets in the Old Testament, has been read by millions of people through all the generations since its composition. No other book has been read so widely and commented on so much. Nevertheless, the fact that catastrophes took place at the time of the Exodus and then again in the eighth century before the present era and the beginning of the seventh, in the time of the prophets Isaiah, Joel, Micah, Nahum, Hosea, Amos and Habakkuk—all of whom speak insistently about these catastrophes—has gone as if unnoticed. The texts are read and looked upon as mere metaphors or allegories of political events. A great fear is manifested in this unwillingness to take notice of the true concern and anxiety of the prophets.

EARLY ATTEMPTS AT RATIONALIZING

With Aristotle (−384 to −322), there came a codification of the oblivion assigned to the natural revolutions that occurred in the historical past: the negation of such events became a statute not only for philosophy but for religion and science as well—and a dogma for political credo. But even before the codification there was an early tendency toward the process of obliteration. One of the mechanisms of obliteration was what we shall call rationalization, or substituting for the unusual what appeared to be less unusual.

One hundred years before Aristotle wrote his codification (never, or hardly ever, challenged in science), Herodotus visited Egypt and wrote down what he heard from the Egyptian priests and from the guides to visitors from other countries.

As I was able to deduce from a multitude of sources from many parts of the world, the last major catastrophe took place on the twenty-third of March, −687 of the Julian calendar.[4] This was the night the army of Sennacherib was destroyed by a "blast," according to the Scriptures and the old Midrashim. But Herodotus heard from the Egyptians that when their king Sethos went with a weak army to Palestine to confront the Assyrians and their king Sennacherib, a multitude of field mice invaded the Assyrian camp during the night and gnawed away the strings of their bows so that the army, now disarmed, fled. Herodotus also added: "And at this day a stone statue of the king (Sethos) stands in Hephaestus' temple, and a mouse in his hand, and an inscription to this effect: 'Look on me, and fear the gods.'"

The event was actually caused by a close approach of the planet Mars, displaced from its earlier orbit by Venus, in the latter's process of joining the planetary family. Although the Chinese records for the night of March 23, −687, tell of a star falling in a rain of shooting stars,[5] the scriptural and more detailed Midrashic sources speak of a fiery blast, the warriors' breath having been extinguished, their clothes, however, having remained unconsumed.[6] The event itself was accompanied by a very loud noise. In *Worlds in Collision* I offered the surmise that "if for some reason the charge of the ionosphere, the electrified layer of the upper atmosphere, should be sufficiently increased, a discharge would occur between the upper atmosphere and the ground, and a thunderbolt would crash from a cloudless sky."[7]

Such an event is not "legal" in Aristotelian or uniformitarian thinking: therefore it not only could not have taken place, but should not even be mentioned. Yet its replacement or rationalization by the story of invading hordes of field mice who in a single night selectively gnawed away the

[4] *Worlds in Collision*, Part II "Mars"; Section "The Year −687".

[5] E. Biot, *Catalogue général des étoiles filantes et des autres météores observés en Chine après le VIIe siècle avant J.C.* (Paris, 1846).

[6] *Worlds in Collision*, Section "Ignis e Coelo."

[7] Ibid., Section "Sword Time, Wolf Time."

strings of the bows, the Assyrian army watching the disaster and succumbing to it—this kind of rationalization does nothing else but strain the imagination.

The obvious irrationality of the rationalization compelled chroniclers to look for a more plausible explanation. Since it is known that bubonic plague is transferred by rats, the mice were replaced by rats, and the army of Sennacherib, it is explained in books on history and theology alike, perished from bubonic plague. To support this view it is pointed out that Apollo Smintheus (Apollo of the Mouse) sends and stays the plague in the *Iliad* (Book I).

"This is Herodotus' version of the Jewish story of the pestilence which destroyed the Assyrian army before Jerusalem," wrote a translator of Herodotus.[8] But none of the ancient Hebrew sources (Scriptures and Midrashim) made any such claim, even though pestilence was rampant and was ascribed to the same disturbances in nature.

The scriptural texts made the event appear as instantaneous.[9] Yet it would require far more than one night for a bubonic plague, or any other plague, to put to death an army of 185,000 men, the number given in the Scriptures.

Interdisciplinary synthesis, or an approach to a subject from more than one discipline, will help to demonstrate how a phenomenon directly related to planetary disaster can come to be paraded as miraculous, rather than involving a derangement of the imperturbable order in the solar system.

Thus in *Worlds in Collision*, in a later chapter, I narrated a tale told by the Menomini Indians, an Algonquin tribe: "The little boy made a noose and stretched it across the path, and when the Sun came to that point the noose caught him around the neck and began to choke him, until he almost lost his breath. It became dark." The Sun cried for

[8] A. D. Godley, note to Book II. 141 (Loeb Classical Library, 1921).
[9] II Kings 19:35; II Chronicles 32:21.

help, but no one who tried could help—"the thread had so cut into the flesh of the Sun's neck that they could not sever it." Then "the Sun called to the mouse to try to cut the string. The mouse came up and gnawed at the string, but it was difficult work, because the string was hot and deeply embedded in the Sun's neck. After working at the string a good while, however, the mouse succeeded in cutting it, when the Sun breathed again and the darkness disappeared. If the mouse had not succeeded the Sun would have died."[10]

Now we have before us two stories in both of which the "savior" is a mouse gnawing a string. But in the Indian story the string disrupted the movement of the Sun. Have the two stories, perchance, no relation one to another?

In Herodotus the famous sentence telling the great secret he learned from the Egyptian priests, that since Egypt became a kingdom the Sun several times changed its wonted path, is found in no other place in his *History* except immediately, actually abruptly, following the story of the debacle of the army of Sennacherib. The same sequence is found in II Kings: the story of Sennacherib in Chapter 19 is followed in Chapter 20 by the account of a disturbance in the movement of the Sun—the Sun's movement retreated on the solar clock ten degrees.

We can learn from these three variants—the one told by Herodotus in the name of the Egyptian priests and the second told by the Algonquin Indians, compared to the third preserved in the Scriptures (Isaiah 36–38, II Kings 18–20 and II Chronicles 32)—how man disfigures the past to purge it of anything that violates his need to have harmony and stability, to have "the heavens themselves, the planets, and this centre, observe degree, priority and place."[11]

[10] *Worlds in Collision*, Section "The Subjective Interpretation of Events and their Authenticity."

[11] Shakespeare, *Troilus and Cressida*, Act I.

Herodotus, visiting Egypt in ca. −450, less than 250 years after the event of March 23, −687, is unaware of accounts in his own country of disturbances in the motion of the Sun—or he writes them off as fables, not worthy of entry in his book of history.

Egyptian priests, though knowing of the repeated reversals of solar motion, confabulated the story of field mice that gnawed the bowstrings, dissociating the event of Sennacherib's debacle from any disarray in the solar motion.

The American Indians preserved the memory of what took place when the distended atmosphere of a celestial body took on the form of a quadruped releasing the Sun that appeared as if snared on a long string—but they made the snarer a little boy, thus depriving the story of its true dramatic elements.

Other tribes, especially of the South and North Pacific, ascribed the "snaring" of the Sun to a demigod. The accounts are presented in *Worlds in Collision*.

By contraposing this material we may learn also why Apollo of the Greeks carried a descriptive adjective *Smintheus*—"of the mouse"—and come closer to the understanding of Apollo himself.

But the main thing we may learn is that the process of rationalization set in only generations away from the events that disturbed that which should never be disturbed.

PLATO

In the preceding section we saw the oblivion in the process of setting in not too long after one of the natural disasters, actually the last. But simultaneously with the phenomenon of incipient, almost willful, amnesia, one can observe an opposite current, a conscious effort to preserve the memory of events that shook the framework of the earth, events in which the entirety of nature—sea and land, Sun and Moon, and all the celestial host—participated.

Fifty years after Herodotus visited Egypt, Plato came there, hardly thirty years of age, soon after having parted from Socrates, who drank his cup of hemlock. When Plato was about ten years old he heard what Solon, generations earlier, had learned from the priests of Sais in Egypt about the cataclysms of the past, one of which caused the destruction and submersion of Atlantis.

Plato lived from ca. −427 to −347, and the last global paroxysm preceded his time by less than three centuries. The disturbances in the motion of the Sun must have been a subject familiar to anyone who read Sophocles' historical drama *Atreus,* of which today but a short fragment is extant. The Sun has risen in the east only since its course was reversed:

Zeus . . . changed the course of the Sun, causing it to rise in the east and not in the west.

Also the readers of Euripides or the theatergoing public knew the passage in the *Electra:*

Then in his wrath arose Zeus, turning the stars' feet back on the fire-fretted way. . . . The Sun . . . turned backward . . . with the scourge of his wrath in affliction repaying mortals.

Stoic philosophers taught the recurrent conflagrations of the world; the Pythagoreans were immersed in speculations of cosmic order and disorder; and before them, in Homer's *Iliad,* there are numerous scenes of theomachy, or war among the planetary gods. The entire Greek pantheon is but a pandemonium on Olympus; and Mount Olympus, in later times located in several vicinities of Greek lands, was originally but the vault of the sky.

It is therefore not surprising to find in Plato a number of passages dealing with the subject of global or even cosmic upheavals. I have quoted from a number of them in *Worlds in Collision*. From *The Statesman* (*Politicus*) I cited Plato's discourse on the reversal of the cardinal points: "I mean the change in the rising and setting of the Sun and other heavenly bodies, how in those times they used to set in the quarter where they now rise, and used to rise where they now set. . . ." With the reversal of the terrestrial axis, the celestial vault is reversed too. Plato continues: "At certain periods the universe has its present circular motion, and at other periods it revolves in the reverse direction. . . . Of all the changes which take place in the heavens this reversal is the greatest and most complete." Such changes were accompanied by decimation and also annihilation of species and genera. "There is at that time great destruction of animals in general, and only a small part of the human race survives."

In the *Timaeus* Plato describes the effects of a collision of the Earth "overtaken by a tempest of winds" with "alien fire from without, and with a solid lump of earth," or by waters of "the immense flood which foamed in and streamed out." The terrestrial globe, disturbed on its path, moved "forwards and backwards, and again to right and to left, and upwards and downwards, wandering every way in all the six directions." The Earth's axis is "at one time reversed, at another oblique, and again upside down." Plato spoke also of cosmic and geophysical disarray with "violent shaking of the revolutions" and "a total blocking of the course" and "shaking of the course" which "produced all manner of twistings, and caused in their circles fractures and disruptures of every possible kind. . . ."

Plato was aware of the process of oblivion that erodes the memory of such paroxysms of nature. In the same *Timaeus*, Plato narrates the visit of Solon of Athens to Egypt, two centuries before Plato's time. I shall follow Francis Cornford's translation:

"Ah, Solon, Solon," said one of the priests, a very old man, "you Greeks are always children; in Greece there is no such thing as an old man."

"What do you mean?" Solon asked.

"You are all young in your minds," said the priest, "which hold no store of old belief based on long tradition, no knowledge hoary with age. The reason is this. There have been, and will be hereafter, many and divers destructions of mankind, the greatest by fire and water, though other lesser ones are due to countless other causes. Thus the story current also in your part of the world, that Phaethon, child of the Sun, once harnessed his father's chariot but could not guide it on his father's course and so burnt up everything on the face of the earth and was himself consumed by the thunderbolt—this legend has the air of a fable; but the truth behind it is a deviation of the bodies that revolve in heaven round the earth and a destruction, occurring at long intervals, of things on earth by a great conflagration. . . . Any great or noble achievement or otherwise exceptional event that has come to pass, either in your parts or here or in any place of which we have tidings, has been written down for ages past in records that are preserved in our temples; whereas with you and other peoples again and again life has only lately been enriched with letters and all the other necessities of civilization when once more, after the usual period of years, the torrents from heaven sweep down like a pestilence, leaving only the rude and unlettered among you. And so you start again like children, knowing nothing of what existed in ancient times here or in your own country. . . . To begin with, your people remember only one deluge, though there were many earlier; and moreover you do not know that the noblest and bravest race in the world once lived in your own country. From a small remnant of their seed you and all your fellow-citizens are derived; but you know nothing of it because the survivors for many generations died leaving no word in writing. . . .

The records tell [that] . . . there was an island in [the Atlantic Ocean] in front of the strait which your countrymen tell me you call the Pillars of Heracles. The island was larger than Libya and Asia [Minor] put together. . . . Now on this Atlantic island there had grown up an extraordinary power under kings who ruled not only the whole island but many of the other islands and parts of the continent; and besides that, within the straits, they were lords of Libya so far as to Egypt, and of Europe to the borders of Tyrrhenia. . . . Afterwards there was a time of inordinate earthquakes and floods; there came one terrible day and night, in which all your men of war were swallowed bodily by the earth, and the island Atlantis also sank beneath the sea and vanished. Hence to this day that outer ocean cannot be crossed or explored, the way being blocked by mud, just below the surface, left by the settling down of the island.[12]

Plato's words "a deviation of the bodies that revolve in heaven round the earth" as the cause of destructions occurring at long intervals need to be emphasized because they are usually overlooked. Innumerable guessers concentrated on "locating" Atlantis in all parts of the world, but not one of them paid attention to these quoted words.

Aristotle was counted among the pupils of Plato. But seen in the proper light, his thesis is the antithesis of Plato's, who sensed the heritage of the ages. Aristotle must have known what Plato wrote and taught. Yet he was singularly disinclined to accept the words of his teacher as anything approaching historical truth. He did not argue against Plato; he just disregarded what his teacher said in so many words in his various works.

[12] F. M. Cornford, *Plato's Cosmology* (The Bobbs-Merrill Co., 1937), pp. 15, 16, 18.

The Aristotelian negation of the traumas of the past, built into a philosophical system that covers many fields of human knowledge, became the rock on which the Alexandrian schools of physics, geometry and astronomy of Archimedes, Euclid and Claudius Ptolemy were built.

The teaching of uniformitarianism (Lyell, Darwin) is a nineteenth-century version of Aristotelianism. And as much as the Church Scientific (Thomas Huxley's expression) still follows in the steps of Darwin, it is still Aristotelian; and, in following Isaac Newton in the study of celestial space and the bodies populating it, the Church Scientific is again Aristotelian. And as much as the latter term is an equivalent of Scholasticism, the Middle Ages are not yet at their end.

ARISTOTLE AND AMNESIA

The following section by Professor Lynn E. Rose was prepared at my suggestion. In it Rose summarizes some of the main themes of his book-in-progress on Aristotle.

Almost every page of the writings of Aristotle raises two nagging questions: (1) "Why would anyone say *that?*" and (2) "Why have people throughout the ages *admired* a person who said such things?" These questions can best be answered in terms of Velikovsky's reconstruction of interplanetary near-collisions and in terms of his concept of collective cultural amnesia.

The core and the frame of Aristotle's system is his cosmology, which not only has been the most influential of all cosmological theories, but also is the most excessive of all such theories in its astronomical uniformitarianism. His views are at the farthest possible extreme from those of Velikovsky; indeed, Aristotle's entire system seems specifically designed to eliminate the very possibility of worlds in collision. That has also been the reason for its enduring popularity and appeal.

Aristotle's cosmological and other ideas were only rarely based on evidence from observation and experience. His ideas seem to have developed largely from his own imagination and from within his own psyche. For what purposes? To gratify personal needs of his own? To serve the political purposes of his Macedonian masters, Philip and Alexander? To eliminate the very possibility of interplanetary near-collisions? It seems very probable that he was often serving all three of these purposes at once. In any case, evidence and argument do not tell the story, and we must turn to psychological considerations if we are to understand the workings of Aristotle's mind.

The case of Aristotle is an excellent one for the application and the illustration of Velikovsky's concept of repressed collective memories of global catastrophes and interplanetary near-collisions, and the ways in which those memories manifest themselves. Indeed, the case history of Aristotle is much more important than any other single such case. It can be argued that *all* of the leading and distinctive features of Aristotle's system served, in one way or another, to soothe Aristotle's deep-seated fear of planetary catastrophes. His denial of what had happened in the past went to such extremes that he created a system in which interplanetary near-collisions not only did not happen, but could not possibly happen. Aristotle and Aristotelianism came to be *the* principal theoretical obstacle to catastrophism. No one, in the entire history of recorded thought, did more than Aristotle in an effort to de-legitimize catastrophism. There is evidence of this not only in the physical and cosmological works, but throughout the Aristotelian corpus.

Aristotle's Earth is at the center of a spherical universe, and is immovable. Within the terrestrial or sublunar realm there is continuing change (this includes coming-to-be and passing-away, as well as changes in quality, quantity, and place), but all such processes are in the long run merely *cyclical*. There is no genuine transition, evolution, or novelty in the terrestrial realm. In the heavens there are fifty-five nested spheres concentric with Earth. These invisible and mathematically perfect spheres are unchangeable and impenetrable: the only "activity" that they are allowed is that of rotation (no other change whatsoever is permitted in the celestial realm).

Aristotle assigns an "intelligence" or guardian angel to each of the fifty-five celestial spheres to keep it moving at an absolutely uniform rate throughout eternity. The poles of each sphere are attached to and carried around by the sphere outside it, in such a way that rather complicated patterns of motion can be reduced to combinations of uniform circular motions. Each of the seven "planets" (Saturn, Jupiter, Mars, Mercury, Venus, the Sun and the Moon) is set like a jewel on the equator of one of the spheres. Each of these planet-bearing spheres is enclosed within layers of other, "unplaneted" spheres. Thus the planets cannot get near each other, any more than they can get near us. Since the planets do not move on their own, but are carried by the spheres, and since the spheres do not move on their own, but are moved by the "intelligences," Aristotle has not only removed the planets two stages from any originating source of motion, but has ensured that the source of motion will be rational rather than blindly irrational.

The *Poetics* might seem an unlikely place to look for Aristotle's reactions to cosmic catastrophes. But we shall see, especially in Aristotle's conception of the ideal tragedy, that the *Poetics* is in many ways an even richer mine of information than are his strictly cosmological works. For Aristotle's cosmology is simply an elaborate denial or repression of the past catastrophes; his philosophy of tragedy, on the other hand, provides him with a way in which he can revisit those catastrophes, safely this time, and with himself in full control. (Both the denial or repression and the revisiting would be at an unconscious level.)

Aristotle emphasizes that tragedy presents "incidents arousing pity and fear, wherewith to accomplish its katharsis of such emotions."[13] But Aristotle's remarks about katharsis or purgation never make it clear whether it is the emotion that is purged of real import, or the spectator who is purged of the emotion. It seems to be the latter sense that Aristotle usually has in mind, but it might also be argued that he intended for "purgation" to apply in both senses: we spectators are purged of the emotions of pity and fear, and the emotions of pity and fear that we feel are themselves purged of the import that they would have if we were viewing real events rather than artificially staged imitations of such events.

Aristotle recognizes various components of tragedy, including plot and character. But it is only the plot, or the arrangement of the incidents, that is crucial:

> But most important of all is the structure of the incidents. . . . Now character determines men's qualities, but it is by their actions that they are happy or the reverse. Dramatic action, therefore, is not with a view to the representation of character; character comes in as subsidiary to the actions. . . . Again, without action there cannot be a tragedy; there may be without character. (1450a15–25)

Aristotle calls special attention to three features of the plot. These are the peripety or reversal of the situation; the recognition; and the pathos or scene of suffering. Aristotle's preference is that the reversal of the situation and the recog-

---

[13] *Poetics* 1449b; the Butcher-Nahm translation.

nition should coincide (as they do in the *Oedipus Tyrannus* of Sophocles).

It is often said that "character is fate." But the fate of a tragic victim, as Aristotle sees it, is a result of the sequence of events, and is not essentially a matter of character. Later theories of tragedy emphasize the "tragic flaw" of the victim. This tragic flaw *is* usually a matter of character, and is often a matter of immorality or vice: the tragic downfall is seen as a consequence of the guilt or mania or other personal trait of the main character. The plot is still important, of course, but it is difficult to see how any proponents of the "character is fate" or "tragic flaw" schools of interpretation could ever agree with Aristotle that the plot alone—that is, the action, the sequence of incidents and events—is what is essential to tragedy, and that there could be tragedy even if there were no character involved. Aristotle is quite explicit that the downfall is "unmerited" (1453a4–5) and that the victim is "like ourselves" (1453a5–6) one "who is not eminently good and just, yet whose misfortune is brought about not by vice or depravity, but by some error or frailty" (1453a8–10). The single Greek word that Butcher translates as "error frailty" is *hamartia*. Aristotle does speak at some length about goodness and badness in victims of tragedy, but it must be stressed that he does not present the moral condition of the victims as a *reason* for their downfalls: all he says is that if the victims are either too bad or too good, we feel no tragic fear or pity. In order for us in the audience to feel pity and fear, we must see the downfall as "unmerited" and we must see the victims as "like ourselves," that is, neither exceptionally good nor exceptionally bad. These are the only considerations that lead Aristotle to mention the moral status of the tragic victims.

In *Poetics*, Aristotle unconsciously models the characteristics of his ideal of tragedy after the characteristics of

cosmic near-collisions. The victims of such cosmic catastrophes (like the tragic victims) are selected independently
of any wrongdoing. Their downfalls are "unmerited" and
come "by surprise." Their fates befall them from outside,
and their characters have nothing to do with it. The main
destruction tends "to confine itself to a single revolution of
the sun, or but slightly to exceed this limit" (1449b13), in
Aristotle's words concerning the dramatic duration of tragedy. (It is noteworthy that Aristotle relates this to the Sun:
he could have simply said "a day or so" without mentioning
a heavenly body at all.) Aristotle's conception of the ideal
tragedy preserves these and—as we shall see—other features
of a cosmic cataclysm. He leaves out of the picture such
considerations as guilt or punishment.

"These then are the rules the poet should observe"
(1454b15), says Aristotle. One wonders if Aristotle has not
left himself open to the same sorts of charges that Glaucon
made against certain critics and that Aristotle strongly en-
dorses:

> Critics, [Glaucon] says, jump at certain groundless conclu-
> sions; they pass adverse judgement and then proceed to rea-
> son on it; and, assuming that the poet has said whatever
> they happen to think, find fault if a thing is inconsistent
> with their own fancy. (1461b1–3)

Aristotle himself points out how rich and varied Greek
tragedy was, and how many were the discrepancies between
what he wanted and what was actually being done in the
theater. Most of it just did not fit the mold that he sought to
impose. The *Poetics* is full of allusions to those in the century or two before Aristotle who did not write as he would
have liked. Aristotle himself seems time after time to "find
fault if a thing is inconsistent with [his] own fancy." (The
Oedipus Tyrannus of Sophocles seems to be Aristotle's fa-
vorite tragedy, one of the very few that he does not criti-

cize.) Aristotle is very narrow in his prescriptions, and he rules out much of what had been done before his time, as well as much of what was to be done after his time. Antigone, for example, was probably *too good* to meet Aristotle's requirements. Clytemnestra, on the other hand, who is the real "protagonist" of the *Agamemnon* of Aeschylus, and who appears in other plays as well, was probably *not good enough* for Aristotle's purposes. And it has often been noted that Aristotle's criteria would exclude such later tragedies as Shakespeare's *Richard III* or *Macbeth*, in which the central characters are evil. Perhaps there are numerous people who are closer to Aristotle in their thinking about tragedy than they would be if he had never lived; but very few accept the entire Aristotelian account, because that would mean that too many excellent tragedies would have to be discarded as inferior.

All of the distinctive features of Aristotle's theory of tragedy were attractive to him for reasons of which he was not conscious—that is, because they all pertain, in one way or another, to interplanetary near-collisions. The victims of planetary catastrophes are, typically, "like ourselves," neither exceptionally virtuous, nor exceptionally vicious. And for that matter they are neither all fit nor all unfit, for the fit suffer no less than the unfit in planetary catastrophes;[14] all are frail reeds. Furthermore, the fate of the victims is unrelated to any tragic flaw in their characters: their fate is "unmerited" and befalls them "by surprise." For most people, the recognition of the near approach of a planetary deity and the peripetous collapse of their worlds coincided, and their tragic stories were finished within "a single revolution of the sun." Thus recognition and peripety come together in a cosmic cataclysm: except for an occasional figure

[14] Velikovsky, *Earth in Upheaval*, page 228: "Fit and unfit, and mostly fit. . . ."

like Isaiah (who was probably only guessing), people did not recognize that another planet was approaching until it was upon them. And we certainly can feel "pity" for the victims of catastrophes and feel "fear" that the same thing might befall us: their vulnerability and frailty is fearfully like our own.

Aristotle was born barely three centuries after the last of the interplanetary near-collisions, and the human species in general had not yet succeeded in submerging its recollections of those catastrophes into the collective unconscious. Plato, in fact, had preserved and endorsed many of the accounts of such catastrophes, accounts that Aristotle and his admirers were soon to reclassify as "mythical" or "unscientific" or "nonhistorical." One function of myth in Plato was to communicate a truth that could not readily be communicated in any other way: "myth" was not a dirty word to Plato. Another function of myth was to preserve an account of past historical events: such an account was basically factual, not fictional. But in Aristotle, myth becomes merely a part of literature; it is fiction, not fact, and is no longer a part of history. Aristotle uses myth as a vehicle through which to ease the tensions that result from his denial of historical truth; the noble myths become mere receptacles for emotional katharsis.

THE ROMAN PHILOSOPHERS

In the last century before the present era, Lucretius knew about the catastrophes and wrote about them in his *On the Nature of Things*. His contemporary, Cicero, the statesman and philosopher of republican Rome, denied the possibility of the planets changing their courses, and declared them to be gods. The divinity of the planets he explained by their occupying the sublime positions and by their unerringly following their paths.

"Therefore the existence of the gods is so manifest that I can scarcely deem one who denies it to be of sound mind."[15]

This dogmatic thinking, changing the statute of faith but not the mode of thinking, existed in all ages: in the Rome of Cicero and Caesar, in Rome of the Catholic Church, in observatories of the present day. The categorical manner in which the dissidents are castigated as being of unsound and vicious mind can be seen again in the burning of Giordano Bruno, and in the compelling of Galileo to recant on his knees—and even in the coercing of the publisher of *Worlds in Collision* to give up the publication.

The notion expressed by Cicero that planets are divine bodies endowed with divine intelligence was deduced not from the fact of their occupying the ethereal heights and moving unerringly; these attributes were called upon only to prove the existing idea of planets and stars being gods. And the source of this belief, deep-rooted and widespread, was in memories of natural phenomena and extraordinary events of the past that grew dimmer with every passing generation.

Pliny, the Roman naturalist of the first century, could tell of interplanetary discharges: "Heavenly fire is spit forth by the planet as crackling charcoal flies from a burning log."[16] Interplanetary thunderbolts, according to him, have been caused in the past by each of the three outer planets, Mars, Jupiter and Saturn.

Seneca, the contemporary of Pliny, mentor of Nero and philosopher, wrote that "the five visible planets are not the only stars with erratic courses, but merely the only ones of the class that have been observed. But innumerable others

---

[15] Cicero, *De Natura Deorum*, translated by H. Rackham (Loeb Classical Library, 1933), II. 1.

[16] *Natural History*, translated by H. Rackham (Loeb Classical Library, 1938), II. 18.

revolve in secret, unknown to us, either by the faintness of their light, or the situation of their orbit being such that they become visible only while they reach its extremities."

"The day will yet come," wrote Seneca in his treatise *De Cometis*, "when the progress of research through long ages will reveal to sight the mysteries of nature that are now concealed. A single lifetime, though it were wholly devoted to the study of the sky, does not suffice for the investigation of problems of such complexity. . . . It must, therefore, require long successive ages to unfold all. The day will yet come when posterity will be amazed that we remained ignorant of things that will to them seem so plain. The five planets are constantly thrusting themselves on our notice; they meet us in all the different quarters of the sky with a positive challenge to our curiosity. . . .

"Many discoveries are reserved for the ages still to be when our memory shall have perished. The world is a poor affair if it does not contain matter for investigation for the whole world in every age. . . . Nature does not reveal all her secrets at once. We imagine we are initiated in her mysteries. We are as yet but hanging around her outer courts."[17]

THE RISE OF ARISTOTELIANISM

The Dark Ages in Europe is the designation of the period from the conquest of Rome by the Goths and Vandals in the fifth century to the beginning of the Renaissance and Reformation in the fifteenth. In learning it was the time of Scholasticism, or the domination of the mind by the teachings of Aristotle. In Moslem countries, however, the Renaissance arrived several centuries earlier.

Three forces kept science from progressing and brought

[17] Seneca, *Quaestiones Naturales*, translated by J. Clarke (London, 1910), pp. 298 ff.

about the Dark Ages: the invasion of the hordes coming from the east and north; the influence of the Church, which imposed dogmas and fettered the human spirit; and the scientific dogma that petrified itself in a thousand-year-long worship of Aristotle—through all the years of the Middle Ages, with their crusades, Scholasticism and Black Death.

A strange amalgam of the Christian dogma and Aristotelianism became the credo of the Church, which regarded the world as finite, and earth as the center of the universe and immovable. The codification in the science of astronomy was performed by a distant pupil of Aristotle, Claudius Ptolemy, an Alexandrian astronomer and mathematician, the greatest authority in those sciences during his own age; through all successive centuries until the time of Tycho de Brahe and Johannes Kepler, almost fifteen hundred years later, it was the undisputed dogma.

Islam spread to Spain in the West and to Bukhara and Kashmir in the East. The Catholic Church dominated Western Europe. America was not yet discovered. In both West and East the Jews, a small dispersed minority, kept their ancient faith from which originally had sprung both Christianity and Islam.

In the twelfth century Averrhoes (1126–98), a learned Muslim and physician in Spain, wrote Aristotelian *Commentaries* and fused Islam with Aristotle; since then this fusion has become inseparable. Moshe ben Maimon, known as Maimonides (1135–1204), who was born in Spain but lived and practiced medicine in Cairo, wrote *The Guide of the Perplexed* and fused rabbinical Judaism with Aristotelianism. These two contemporaries, born nine years apart, were followed by Thomas Aquinas (1224–74), a Dominican monk, who wrote *Summa Theologica* and fused Catholicism with Aristotelianism.

These three are regarded as the greatest authorities in the theologies of their respective religions, and by their time the cosmic events in historical times had become misinterpreted as metaphors: the Scriptures were censored.[18] The true miracles of unchained elements, the resurgent chaos, the awe, were denied emergence into the conscious mind.

COPERNICUS

Eighteen hundred years passed after the time of Aristotle and thirteen and a half centuries after the days of Claudius Ptolemy, and their teaching of the spheres revolving around the Earth in the center of the universe survived unaltered, and not only survived but dominated unchallenged. Universities of the Middle Ages and the Church with its philosophers and theologians kept dogmatically to this doctrine.

In 1492, when Columbus discovered the West Indies of the Americas, Nicolaus Copernicus was a youth of eighteen years, enrolled at the University of Krakow. He further pursued his studies in Italy, then returned to his native Poland to become canon of the town of Frauenburg.

In 1506 or 1507, Copernicus began to work on his *De Revolutionibus Orbium Coelestium* (*Of the Revolutions of the Celestial Orbs*). He showed that the Sun, and not the Earth, occupies the center of the universe, and demonstrated that the Earth rotates in a daily motion and revolves in a yearly motion. He did not, however, part with the concept of uniform circular motion, nor did he understand the nature of the fixed stars—great suns at immense distances—regarding them as lights attached to an enormous sphere that constituted the boundary of the universe.

In the 1530s, Martin Luther, who in 1517 had first broken with the pope, came out against Copernicus, assailing the "new astrologer who wanted to prove that the Earth was

[18] Velikovsky, *Worlds in Collision*, Section "Maimonides and Spinoza, the Exegetes."

moving and revolving rather than heaven or the whole
firmament, Sun and Moon. . . . this fool wants to turn the
whole art of astronomy upside down. But as the Holy Scrip-
ture testifies, Joshua ordered the Sun to stand still, not the
Earth!" Along with his rebellion against the Roman Church,
he spurned the revolutionary of the starry sky.

In the Preface to his *De Revolutionibus* Copernicus
wrote:

> I can easily conceive . . . that as soon as some people
> learn that in this book which I have written concerning the
> revolutions of the heavenly bodies, I ascribe certain motions
> to the Earth, they will cry out at once that I and my theory
> should be rejected. Accordingly, when I considered in my
> own mind how absurd a performance it might seem to those
> who know that the judgement of many centuries has ap-
> proved the view that the Earth remains fixed as center in
> the midst of heaven, if I should on the contrary assert that
> the Earth moves—when I considered this carefully, the con-
> tempt which I had to fear because of the novelty and appar-
> ent absurdity of my view, nearly induced me to abandon the
> work I had begun. How did it occur to me to venture, con-
> trary to the accepted view of mathematicians, and well-nigh
> contrary to common sense, to form any conception of any
> terrestrial motion whatsoever?

Copernicus kept postponing the publication of his work
until he saw his days declining and a lasting night approaching. Then he feared to appear before his Lord without having told to men on Earth the truth disclosed to him. After
decades of postponement he was persuaded by his only
pupil, Rheticus, to permit him to publish his work, *De Revolutionibus*. On May 24, 1543, a few hours before Copernicus
died the first copy was put in his hands.

What is it that was so unacceptable in the heliocentric
system? It is that man needs the feeling of security, a need

based most probably on a hidden insecurity. A moving earth is a less secure place than an unmovable one. Moreover, the system denied man the central role in the universe; this was injurious to his ego. It was also in conflict with the tenets of the Christian Church; did Jesus come merely to a very secondary planet, one of many?

But among these considerations, mainly the awakened feeling of insecurity was at the basis of the great anguish that greeted the retarded announcement of the Copernican theory. The great derailment of this planet on its travels put a deep-seated fear into man's soul; and as the deepest traumas are relegated to oblivion in the soul of a single individual, so also is the case with humankind.

GALILEO AND GIORDANO

When Galileo embraced the Copernican doctrine of the Earth and other planets revolving around the Sun, he broke not with the Scriptures, but with Aristotle. The Inquisition interrogated him on his rejection of the dogma of the Earth as the central body, the Sun with other planets revolving around it, which is the Aristotelian teaching, not the scriptural. The possibly apocryphal words of Galileo, rising from his knees after recanting: *"Eppur si muove!"* (And yet it moves!) reflect the issue and the content of the crime. Only in the opening chapter does the Old Testament appear to let the Sun serve to illuminate the Earth for man's sake. The rest of the Old Testament speaks repeatedly of such events as the Earth removed from its place, or overturned—ideas illegitimate in the codex of Aristotle. Actually, the Church as the trustee of both the Scriptures and of Aristotle accepted the latter almost straight, but with respect to the Scriptures the Church devised a metamorphosis of the grandiose miracles of nature, changing them into personal miracles of saints.

Galileo, himself a devout Catholic, made this sole deviation from Aristotle—actually the deviation of the canon Copernicus, whose work was published ninety years before Galileo was brought before the Inquisition (1633). Galileo did not dare to break as decisively as his contemporary, the Protestant Johannes Kepler, who abandoned circular orbits and introduced elliptical ones, or as completely as their early contemporary, the pantheist Giordano Bruno, who removed both the Sun and the Earth from their exalted positions by pronouncing the fixed stars to be suns, themselves surrounded by planets.

Galileo and Giordano were punished according to their trespasses: Galileo to eighteen days in the prison of the Inquisition and house arrest till the end of his life; Giordano Bruno to over seven years' imprisonment and death at the stake. Bruno, however, renounced not only the Aristotelian immovable Earth in the center of the universe, but also the dogma of the Immaculate Conception. This he had done early in his life, when he deserted his cell in the Dominican monastery at Nola on the slopes of Vesuvius—a cell once occupied, three centuries earlier, by Thomas Aquinas. Bruno's heresy was against both doctrines welded together by Thomas, and on February 17, 1600, from the pile of faggots kindled on Campo dei Fiori in Rome, he was sent to the Inferno by the Inquisition.[19]

NICOLAS-ANTOINE BOULANGER

The name Nicolas-Antoine Boulanger is not found in most encyclopedias and is known only to a few scholars. He was a

[19] Antoinette Mann Paterson, *The Infinite Worlds of Giordano Bruno* (C. C. Thomas, 1970).

contemporary of Jean-Jacques Rousseau, Voltaire and Diderot, illustrious names in the history of French letters. He lived only thirty-seven years, from 1722 to 1759. I came across the name very late in my research, actually in 1963,[20] and read in his works a few years later. I found that in some aspects he was the precursor of Freud and Jung as well as of myself, actually solving the problem Freud and Jung left unsolved. Namely, he understood that much of the behavior of the human species, together with all the heritage of religious rites and much of the political structure of his own and other ages, were engendered in cataclysmic experiences of the past, in the Deluge (or deluges, of which there could have been more than one).

After Boulanger's premature death, his works were published by Diderot, but his geological observations were not included in the printed volumes; extracts from these observations and reflections appear in a recent work on Boulanger,[21] and do not impress as compelling. But one has to keep in mind that the age of geology as a science did not start until after Boulanger's death.

In Boulanger's time, geology as a science was in a prenatal stage. But as a road engineer, his observations in the valley of the Marne made him draw conclusions which he found substantiated in the existing books of folklore and sacred writings by the classical writers available to him either in originals or in translation. He was convinced that the Deluge was a global occurrence, although this was no innovation on his part but an accepted notion in his time. Boulanger, in fact, was the author of the entry *Déluge* in the great French *Encyclopédie* edited by Diderot. In his books he sometimes referred to the Deluge as a singular occur-

[20] First in the paper by Livio Stecchini, "The Inconstant Heavens," in *American Behavioral Scientist*, September 1963, p. 30.

[21] J. Hampton, *Nicolas-Antoine Boulanger et la science de son temps* (Geneva-Lille, 1955).

rence, but then again he spoke of multiple deluges. He seems not to have had an idea where the water of the universal flood might have come from, and showed no awareness of any extraterrestrial agent having caused the worldwide calamity: none of the planets figures in his work as involved in the upheaval. Neither did he connect the description of the events surrounding the Exodus with a catastrophic happening, nor did he arrive at the conclusion that the speeches of the Hebrew prophets in the days of the Assyrian domination (eighth century before the present era) dealt with contemporaneous global upheavals. Nevertheless he was ready to claim, at least on one occasion, that only three thousand years had passed since order was established in nature. Thus human beings must have witnessed these upheavals; the human race suffered one or several violent experiences, whose aftereffects are still with us:

"We still tremble today from the consequences of the deluge, and our institutions, without our knowing it, still pass on to us the fears and the apocalyptic ideas of our forefathers. Terror subsists from race to race, and the experience of the centuries can only weaken it but cannot make it entirely disappear. The child will fear forever what frightened his ancestors."[22]

In the broad generalization that our society, as well as the savage society, still lives in the shadow of the experience of the Deluge, Boulanger anticipated Jung and Freud and spelled out the nature of this experience that influenced the behavior of the subsequent generations. Frank E. Manuel maintains that in Boulanger's conception "there is no physiological transmission of the postdiluvian terror, nor a theological incubus of sin, merely a historical tradition embodied in rites, myths, ceremonials. Boulanger required no biologi-

[22] Nicolas-Antoine Boulanger, *L'antiquité dévoilée par ses usages* (Amsterdam, 1766), Bk. 6, ch. 2.

cal mechanism or race memory plasmically inherited to account for the enduring effects of the trauma of the flood; mere imitation and institutional inheritance was adequate, a theory which allowed also for the relatively easy cure of the disease and thus generated an optimism whose spirit is to be distinguished from the traumatized humanity of Freud."[23]

Neither Freud nor Jung knew anything of Boulanger, and his name is not found in the psychological literature. It is not so much his claim that catastrophic events took place in the past that deserves attention; rather, Boulanger's distinction lies in his contemplating the consequences of such upheavals for the human race. The idea of catastrophic events in the past was already to be found in the writings of William Whiston, successor to Isaac Newton in Trinity College, Cambridge, who claimed that the Deluge was caused by a comet that returned in his own time, in 1680; again, Georges Louis de Buffon, Boulanger's contemporary, thought that a massive comet hit the Sun and caused the origin of the planetary family; and after Boulanger's time the scientific thought of the eighteenth century and the first half of the nineteenth again and again sought the cause of the global upheavals.

LAPLACE'S DICHOTOMY

In his *Traité de mécanique céleste* (1779–1825) Pierre Simon de Laplace proved that the solar system, governed by gravitation, is orderly and that the planets move on eternally peaceful orbits. In his *Exposition du système du monde* (1796), discussing the possibility of a collision of the Earth with a comet, he began by belittling the chance and the result, but as he continued he became noticeably inspired, and soon admitted the possibility of a horrendous effect. Next he claimed that many problems of geology and of ancient climate must have had their explanations in exactly such an event. Thus Laplace displayed a dichotomy: he denied the possibility of disturbances in the solar system of such magnitude, and at the same time he confessed belief in the actuality of such events.

His claim that the solar system was not and cannot be disturbed is well known, and this basic credo of modern astronomy is so often quoted that it is not necessary to cite Laplace on this score. As to the other statement, since reference to it is systematically omitted from the scientific literature, I shall reproduce it here. Should a comet of the mass of the Earth pass close by,

the axis and the movement of rotation would be changed. The seas would abandon their ancient positions, in order to precipitate themselves toward the new equator; a great portion of the human race and the animals would be drowned in the universal deluge, or destroyed by the violent shock imparted to the terrestrial globe; entire species would be annihilated; all monuments of human industry overthrown; such are the disasters which the shock of a comet would produce, if its mass were comparable to that of the earth.

We see then, in effect, why the ocean has receded from the high mountains, upon which it has left incontestable marks of its sojourn. We see how the animals and plants of the south have been able to exist in the climate of the north, where their remains and imprints have been discovered; finally, it explains the newness of the human civilization, certain monuments of which do not go further back than five thousand years. The human race, reduced to a small number of individuals, and to the most deplorable state, solely occupied for a length of time with the care of its own preservation, must have lost entirely the remembrance of the sciences and the arts; and when progress of civilization made these wants felt anew, it was necessary to begin again, as if man had been newly placed upon the earth.[24]

I cite this passage of Laplace to illustrate a state of split personality, not just of this savant, regarded as the genius who brought the Newtonian system to its perfection, but also of those who now, for almost two hundred years, have preferred the fairy tale of a blissful world to the shocking record of an earth in upheaval.

At the biennial meeting of the American Philosophical Society convened at Notre Dame University, in Indiana, on November 2, 1974, I spoke of the desire of science to know, and the equally strong desire not to know. Since Aristotle in classical times, and Laplace in modern times, the desire to know only so much and not more has dominated scientific endeavor.

DARWIN

The extent to which the fear of recognition that we travel on an accident-prone vessel governs the thinking of modern science can be exemplified by a few instances.

Charles Darwin, as a young naturalist, visited South America; it was in fact the scene of his by-far-longest stay in the course of the circumterrestrial voyage on the ship *Beagle*. He wrote in his *Journal* of his voyage (I have also quoted the passages in *Earth in Upheaval*): "It is impossible to reflect on the changed state of the American continent without the deepest astonishment. Formerly it must have swarmed with great monsters: now we find mere pigmies, compared with the antecedent, allied races."

He continued: "The greater number, if not all, of these

[24] *Oeuvres complètes de Laplace*, 6th edition (Paris, 1835), pp. 234–35.

extinct quadrupeds lived at a late period, and were the contemporaries of most of the existing sea-shells. Since they
lived, no very great change in the form of the land can have
taken place. What, then, has exterminated so many species
and whole genera? The mind at first is irresistibly hurried
into the belief of some great catastrophe; but thus to destroy
animals, both large and small, in Southern Patagonia, in
Brazil, on the Cordillera of Peru, in North America up to
Behring's Straits, *we must shake the entire framework of the
globe.*" (Italics added.)

Darwin did not know the answer and he wrote: "It could
hardly have been a change of temperature, which at about
the same time destroyed the inhabitants of tropical, temper-
ate, and arctic latitudes on both sides of the globe." It was
not man who acted as a destroyer; and were he to attack all
large animals, would he also, Darwin asked, be the cause of
extinction "of the many fossil mice and other small quadrupeds . . ."? Darwin concluded: "Certainly, no fact in
the long history of the world is so startling as the wide and
repeated exterminations of its inhabitants."[25]

Having seen what he did in South America, Darwin could
not but embrace catastrophism. He did not come by his information through mere reading: he saw the very remains of
catastrophe victims, not in museums, but *in situ*, in the
pampas and on the slopes of the Andes. Such an experience
is more compelling than literary information. Yet, two decades later Darwin propounded a non sequitur in ascribing
all changes in the animal kingdom to a very slow evolution
through competition, and by an extended dialectic he en-

[25] Charles Darwin, *Journal of Researches into the Natural History and
Geology of the Countries Visited During the Voyage of H.M.S. Beagle
Round the World*, under date of January 9, 1834 (New York, London:
Appleton & Co.), pp. 169–70.

deavored to demonstrate that the earth pursued a stable evolution on a stable course of uninterrupted circling, because the idea of a shaking of the entire globe was mentally beyond him. But he saw these animals, their bones splintered, heaped in the strangest assemblages—giant sloths and mastodons together with birds and mice. He had to forget these pictures of disaster in order to invent a theory of a peaceful earth unshaken in its entirety—an earth populated by species competing for livelihood, and benefiting from chance variations, all of them evolving from a few unicellular organisms, as though mere competition ("survival of the fittest") could produce from the same animal ancestor a winged bird, a winding snake, a multilegged insect and man. With our present knowledge of the phenomena of transmutations of elements and biological mutations that take place in extreme conditions, thermal or radioactive, we no longer need subscribe to the idea that eons of competition for the means of existence caused wings to grow on land creatures and the entire population of land, air and water to evolve from a common ancestor. But whatever the cause of evolution—in his time Darwin could not know of the phenomenon of mutation—the phenomenon of destruction of a multitude of genera and species was known to him, and he could not pass over it in silence in the *Origin of Species*. He wrote: "The extinction of species has been involved in the most gratuitous mystery. . . . No one can have marvelled more than I have done at the extinction of species." But then he chose to find an explanation in "wide intervals of time between our consecutive [geological] formations; and in these intervals there may have been much slow extermination."[26]

This explanation, assuming lacunae in the geological record, without which there would have been found evidences

[26] Charles Darwin, *On the Origin of Species*, sixth edition (New York, London: Appleton & Co.), vol. II, pp. 95–96, 99.

of gradual extinction of "unfit" species, does not help to explain the observed hecatombs of animals, not only of extinct species but in a melee with still-extant forms which also succumbed in the same paroxysms of nature. These remains were obviously heaped together in single actions of nature with no geological hiatus intervening. The heaps of perished animals in South America and all over the world were widely known in Darwin's days: Alfred Russel Wallace, who simultaneously with Darwin announced the theory of natural selection, in puzzlement drew the attention of the scientific world to the Siwalik hills, at the foot of the Himalayas, their several hundred miles of length practically packed with bones of animals.

One may frame hypotheses for what one does not see, like the hypothesis of geological gaps, the foundation of the entire *Origin of Species*. But for what one *does* see, the evidence of great cataclysms, it is no explanation to assume a defective geological record.

The Christian Church maintains that animals have no souls and that an unbridgeable gulf exists between the kingdoms of man and animal. When Darwin destroyed the sense of absolute separateness of man and animal, he undermined belief in the soul's being separate from and surviving the body. Thus Darwin deflated man's pride in his origin and uniqueness. But there was another aspect of Darwin's theory, without which the opposition to his teaching would have been much more intense and prolonged. This was a feeling of security about the peaceful history of our planet, the abode of man—no catastrophic interruptions in all the eons of the past and none in the future. For that assurance, man was ready to part with the idea of his uniqueness and agree to be counted as one of the animal kingdom. This did not require his giving up his status as number one, free to exploit and even consume any of his animal brethren, regardless of their position on the ladder of evolution. He did not need to accord franchise to horses or primates: his own female folk were not yet granted voting rights. It was more like finding that the genealogical list one thought to be genuine was actually not so, and the assumed nobility was not based on the ancestors' high ranking; there was no blue blood flowing in the veins of the primates. This loss occasioned the satirical question Bishop Samuel Wilberforce directed to Thomas Huxley during their famous encounter: ". . . was it through your grandfather or your grandmother that you claim to have descended from a monkey?"

So man was offered an opportunity to barter his godlike origin for the security of his abode. Darwin knew the sacrifice (in intangibles) he asked and the guarantee of peace of mind he offered. Who cares for the past if the future is at stake? Darwin made it clear on the concluding page of the *Origin of Species:* "As all the living forms of life are the lineal descendants of those which lived long before the Cambrian epoch, we may feel certain that the ordinary succession by generation has never once been broken, and that no cataclysm has desolated the whole world. Hence we may look forward with some confidence to a secure future of great length."

Darwin ended the *Origin of Species* with these words: "There is grandeur in this view of life, with its several powers, having been originally breathed by the Creator into a few forms or into one; and that, whilst this planet has gone cycling on according to the fixed law of gravity, from so simple a beginning endless forms most beautiful and most wonderful have been, and are being evolved."

The plot now being settled, the drama of everyone against everybody else could go on without any fear that the stage itself would collapse. For man at the top of the ladder it was like a license to devour or exploit the less developed—soul or

no soul; for man, this battle of survival in the animal kingdom is usually no more than sport. In any case, what all this
did was quickly to bestow a century-long enduring victory of
Darwinism over man's hidden apprehension as a descendant
of survivors of catastrophes of unfathomable destructive
power.

NATURAL EVOLUTION AND REVOLUTION

Darwin's *On the Origin of Species by Means of Natural
Selection* appeared in November of 1859 and was an immediate success: on the day of publication, the whole edition
of 1,250 copies was sold out.

In books on the history of science, and more specifically in
books on Darwin, one regularly reads of the bitter opposition the book provoked. This statement needs qualification.
It is true that the great names in science of the time like
Louis Agassiz, the ichthyologist, the botanist Asa Gray and
others expressed upon reflection great reservations at Darwin's views, yet they did so without disrespect and purely
on scientific grounds. Agassiz pointed out that the skeletal
remains of a number of ancient and extinct species of fish
documented a better progression on the road of evolution
and a better adaptation in the struggle for existence than do
later species of fish, and thus the principle of the survival of
the fittest had not been followed through. But the academic
chorus in Darwin's support was heard ever louder, and soon
the spectacle in the intellectual circles was a rush to join the
winning team. Thomas Huxley in England and Ernst
Haeckel in Germany spearheaded the movement. Darwin
kept himself in the background, but occasionally instigated
his front fighters to demolish a scientific opponent, usually
among the clerics, by circumventing scientific argument and
attacking the critic personally, as was the case with a
French savant, St. Georges Mivart, who offered solid ar-

guments against the theory of evolution by natural selection. In his correspondence, Darwin referred to Lamarck, a predecessor in the teaching of evolution, by then long dead, as the author of "that wretched book." Darwin also completely disregarded the work of the founders of the science of geology—Sir Roderick Murchison, William Buckland and Adam Sedgwick—of the early nineteenth century, who gave the names, still in use today, to almost all the geological periods—Cambrian, Permian, Ordovician, Cretaceous, etc. He also circumvented by silence the founder of mammalian paleontology and ichthyology, Georges Cuvier. These founders of earth science produced consistent data showing that catastrophic events on a global scale had repeatedly interrupted the flow of natural history. Darwin followed Charles Lyell, who was a lawyer by education and who argued the theory of uniformity not as a savant, but as a barrister; it was his book which Darwin read when he traveled on the H.M.S. *Beagle* and which, as he acknowledged, was his Bible.

Obviously there was a psychological need in Darwin to shut his eyes to contrary evidence, but also a similar need in both the academic and the lay society to get rid of the natural revolution by embracing natural evolution. One wonders at the avidity displayed by scientists in the acceptance of the Darwinian theory. None of the arguments that could have been used against him was utilized by his opponents. In his published diaries from his travels in South America, for example, a number of entries point to a cataclysmic interruption of the flow of the struggle for existence among life forms. There was not only the instance quoted earlier about the necessity to shake the frame of the entire world to account for the massive and sudden extinction of a multitude of animal species, but also the evidence of a rise of the coast of Chile by over a thousand feet in a period shorter than necessary for seashells to decay, and the repeated transgressions of the ocean all the way across Brazil to the

foothills of the Andes. Yet with no new fieldwork by him between these observations and the *Origin of Species*, he
protested in the latter against catastrophic changes of land
and sea contours, and against any continental, much less
global, upheavals. None of these contradictions between his
diary observations and his views in his major work was raised
by any of his opponents. It was not brought up against him
that he had no academic position in a university, or that his
only scholastic degree was that of a bachelor of theology, or
that he omitted all footnotes to his sources, so that it was
often impossible for a reader to check on the data; none of
these shortcomings was ever mentioned by his critics. In addition to not heeding the solid finds of the still very young
geological and paleontological sciences, Darwin, with all his
entourage of acolytes, failed to learn of the work of his contemporary, Gregor Mendel, who evinced the basic laws of
heredity and prepared the foundation for modern genetics.

Darwin's was the spirit of the Victorian age—an evolutionary theory that was claimed to be a revolution, which it
was not. Darwin became the supreme authority, the symbol
of resolution of all questions, and a substitute for the Creator himself, who had to be suspected of being untrustworthy
if the Mosaic books were inspired by him and the story of
Creation now proved to be a fabrication.

The success of Darwin, the speedy acceptance of his
theory by academia, and the penetration of his theory into
all things spiritual and material of the last hundred years
was due to his assurance that the frame of this globe had
never been shaken.

KARL MARX'S MISAPPREHENSION

Jacques Barzun tells how Marx "wished to dedicate a portion of *Das Kapital* to the author of the *Origin of Species*.

Darwin declined the honor. . . ."[27] In offering to dedicate to Darwin a part of his *Kapital*—the battle cry for the liberation of the "unfit" from exploitation by the "fit"—Marx was pursuing some unclear thinking. By refusing the offer, Darwin was the more logical of the two.

The teaching of Darwin in a sense sanctified the exploitation of the less fit by the better fit—that is, exploitation of those less able to adapt to the circumstances and opportunities of the times. The industrial revolution that was shaping itself in the Victorian age saw the enterprising, but also the unscrupulous, take advantage of the underprivileged, the resourceless, the ignorant, the unprotected—in a word, the unfit. The exploitation manifested itself in work hours from before dawn into the night, in child labor paid pittances, in unhygienic factories and perilous mines. The exploiter cared less for the physical survival of the human animal than for the survival of a field animal: the latter was a property of the owner, but the human animal was easily replaced with no loss to the exploiter.

Marx observed and studied industrial relations, and came out against the fit. The British Islands, having lost the American colonies at the end of the former century, now, under Victoria, were expanding to become the dominant colonial power in the world. The blacks of Africa, the dark-skinned peoples of the lands bordering the Indian Ocean and various other colors were enslaved as colonial people—and though the colonial expansion of the British goes back to the sixteenth century, it never reached the scope, the glamour and the degree of extortion that it did in the days of Victoria. Neither the House of Commons and the House of Lords, nor the Prime Minister and his Cabinet, were in any hurry with legislation for the protection of the exploited at

[27] Jacques Barzun, *Darwin, Marx, Wagner: Critique of a Heritage* (Boston, 1941), p. 10.

home or abroad. Great Britain ruled the seas; the Queen was soon to be proclaimed Empress.

Marx was what the Germans call a *Luftmensch,* a ne'er-do-well. He had no steady occupation, no permanent means of existence. Born in Germany, a migrant to France, then to London, the man with the broad forehead and a lion's mane of hair daily mounted the steps of the library of the British Museum on Russell Square. One after another the children born to him in London died of malnutrition and poor medical care. One day his furniture was put out on the sidewalk for nonpayment of rent. But he doggedly continued his fight for the downtrodden, the unfit. He could have selected his motto from a number of quotes in the Hebrew prophets, wherein, without benefit of labor and finance statistics, they proclaimed the same social imperative. "Woe unto them that join house to house, that lay field to field, till there be no place, that they may be placed alone in the midst of the earth!" (Isaiah 5:8) The prophets were rebels against the throne, the rich, the exploiters.

Marx even looked as we would imagine an Old Testament prophet, notwithstanding his bow tie and the lapels of a formal suit. But he denied all links to the old prophets. His was a materialistic understanding of history. He even dismissed his Jewish origin. At the age of six he had been baptized—and one of his earlier works after he converted to communism was against the Jews.

The modern originator of the idea of communism was Moses Hess, German-born, living and writing in France. To him in 1840 came the young Friedrich Engels, and a year later Engels introduced Marx to Hess's ideas. Several years thereafter they composed *The Communist Manifesto,* and the movement began. Hess, however, soon sensed that the new movement would one day bring hatred and violence, and as if in prophetic anticipation of Stalin's Siberian labor camps and the subjugation of the countries of Eastern Europe, wrote to Alexander Herzen, the Russian emigré and anarchist:

> As you know, I do not deny the possibility of such a death without resurrection, such a definite victory of barbarism and brutality; I only maintain that invasion, barbarism and reaction are so inseparably linked together, that one inevitably brings the others with it. To save your [idea of a] Slavic invasion, the only thing that remains to you is to turn Socialism from what you . . . have made into a negative idea—such as anarchy in the political sphere and atheism in the religious—into a positive idea.[28]

In the year 1862 Hess wrote *Rome and Jerusalem,* a work of reawakened national conscience. He foresaw the huge wave of anti-Semitism that would sweep France with the Dreyfus Affair, and understood the problem of Jews in various nations more penetratingly than Theodor Herzl a generation later. Herzl first thought of salvation for the race in assimilation—but then in the days of the Dreyfus trial wrote his *Jewish State,* not yet specifying where that state was to be.

Karl Marx, still building on Darwin, as Darwin had built on Newton, changed human history, yet neither he nor those who followed him perceived that in the light of historical materialism and in the uproar of political revolution he and they were emulating the natural revolution, not the natural evolution. The excesses of revolution, and later Stalin's purges, debased human beings, deprived them of the natural rights to freedom of thought, expression and change of habitat, and made them into abject slaves. The several hun-

[28] Moses Hess, *Briefwechsel,* edited by E. Silberner (Mouton, 1959), p. 253.

dreds beheaded on the Place de la Concorde in Paris in the days of the French Revolution were followed in a century and a half by millions brought to mock trials, imprisoned, tortured and murdered, with Marx watching from his omnipresent portrait.

The foundation of the Marxian edifice was placed by its author in such a way that it did not reach the bedrock. Hence tribulations and possible collapse endanger the edifice.

The doctrine of the fit, whom natural law expects, almost obliges, to live off the unfit, developed in its next phase into Nietzsche's teaching of the Superman to whom all is permitted. And the basis for the Hitlerian philosophy in the following generation was prepared: out of "fit" and then "Superman" emerged the concept of a master race. Wagnerian brasses called up memories of Nordic Valhallas, and the violence of sword and fire in the Bismarckian military drill impelled the *Drang nach Osten* (drive toward the East). At last the armies, goose-stepping eastward, met their doom as they collided with the other end product of nineteenth-century ideology.

TWO FORMS OF FEAR

A few weeks before World War II started, while in Moscow signatures were being put on a document that unleashed the thrust of the Nazi armies toward East and West, I was with my family on my way to the shores of the New World. During the years of war, powerless to change anything on the world scene, I spent my days in reading, in research, in thinking and in writing.

I would sit at the feet of the sages of many ancient civilizations—one day of the Egyptian learned scribes, another of the Hebrew rabbis, the next of the Hindus, the Chinese or the Pythagoreans. Then I would rise to my feet to confer with present-day scientific knowledge. At times I understood what perplexed the ancients, and at other times I found answers to what perplexes the moderns. This shuttle back and forth was a daily occupation for a decade or more, and it became a way to understand the phenomena: to listen to those who lived close to the events of the past, even to witnesses, and to try to understand them in the light of theoretical and experimental knowledge of the last few centuries, in this manner confronting witnesses and experts.

I realized very soon that the ancient sages lived in a frightened state of mind, justified by the events they or their close ancestors had witnessed. The moderns, however, had to their disadvantage a dogmatic belief in uniformitarianism —a hypothesis raised to the status of a fundamental law, based on the premise that no cataclysmic events ever took part in shaping the world and the life on it. I had to take into account both shortcomings—the fear that often degenerated into the worship of planetary deities, religious wars and superstitions; and the fear that made modern man a dedicated partisan of uniformitarianism: nothing could have taken place in the past that has not taken place before our eyes, in our days, or, say, in the days since Isaac Newton.

The two forms of fear had a common origin, but the latecomers denied their ancestors' wisdom—even their integrity —in that the ancients' message was but an anguished effort to communicate the awe engendered by seeing nature with its elements unchained. The adherence to the dogma of uniformitarianism is a symptom of an all-embracing fear of facing the past, even the historically documented experiences of our progenitors, as recent as four score generations ago.

A CHOICE

The content of *Worlds in Collision* was made known in a summary preview by the writer Eric Larrabee, printed in *Harper's Magazine* for January 1950. Then in the *New Republic* of March 6, 1950, under the title "A Distinct Choice," appeared this piece by Harold Ickes, who served as Secretary of the Interior under Franklin Roosevelt:

We have been worrying to the point of hysteria about Russia loosing a bomb on Washington or New York. Now we can turn our minds to something different.

Dr. Immanuel Velikovsky, one of the founders of the University of Jerusalem, has inspired a terror so beyond imagination that we may be able to shake off such trivial fears as those of the A-bomb and the H-bomb. . . . He quotes from ancient records and legends to prove that, in the wars between Venus and Earth, the latter almost succumbed to the great heat that was engendered. . . . The very title of Dr. Velikovsky's book, *Worlds in Collision,* which will shortly be published, is enough to scare out of us the fears that we have been cherishing. . . . [If another encounter should take place] both Venus and Earth would be chaff in the hands of cosmic forces that are uncontrollable.

In the circumstances it seems more than a little childish for Russia and the United States to continue a race in armaments that would melt into molten metal before the ardency of the amorous Venus. It has happened that enemies can spontaneously become friends when a present danger threatens both. . . . Perhaps, without knowing what he was doing, Dr. Velikovsky has conferred a great boon on all of us. He has given us something to think about; something even to pray about. . . . Perhaps we shall have sense enough to put our heads between our hands and do some real thinking about universal and lasting peace.

. . . A fresh start, dissociated from anything that has happened within the experience of recent generations, might conceivably lead to an accomplishment that is not beyond the reach of imaginative and bold men . . . to live in peace and good fellowship with our neighbors.

The article was written as a feuilleton, and in it the "Old Curmudgeon," as Ickes was called, mixed serious thought with frivolous description of what the Greeks knew as *theomachy*. But the serious side of Ickes' article was much too grim to be appreciated for its stark sense of urgency. Therefore it was regarded as a piece of whimsy rather than a warning to make us really "put our heads between our hands."

The irrationally emotional reaction to *Worlds in Collision* of so many people, especially among scientists, it seemed to me must surely be caused by a hidden fear of knowing the events of the past, more than by an aversion to challenging the conventional notions of science.[29]

"A DEGRADATION OF SCIENCE AND OF RELIGION"

The reaction against efforts to bring to the surface of consciousness repressed contents that struggle to stay repressed can be violent and cause an outburst of hatred; the person trying to help another to bring up the suppressed may himself be accused of fomenting hatred and discord. Hostility against the therapeutical procedure may ascribe to the therapist vile motives actually existing in the analysand himself

[29] I refer the reader to an article by Livio Stecchini, "The Inconstant Heavens," written for the *American Behavioral Scientist*, September 1963, reprinted in *The Velikovsky Affair*, A. de Grazia, ed. (New York, 1966), pp. 80–126. It sheds some light on the motives behind the concerted campaign to suppress my book even before its publication.

under a veneer of conscious reasonableness. An illustrative case is the reaction of the late J.B.S. Haldane upon reading *Worlds in Collision*.

Haldane was a British geneticist who claimed the mantle of a prophet. When *Worlds in Collision* was published in England he wrote a review article in *The New Statesman and Nation* (November 11, 1950). The efforts he exerted to damage *Worlds in Collision* can be discussed under several headings. His scientific arguments need not occupy us here, and they are answered by scientific progress since 1950.

Haldane, among other things, used the technique of associating the book with the greatest terror living in the British nation since the bombing blitz of World War II. He wrote:

> I regard the wide sales which this book has had in the United States as one of the most alarming symptoms of our times. The journals (see list on dust cover) in which it was boosted are those which may urge the use of Britain as a base for atomic warfare. A large section of the American people is dreaming in terms of world disasters, and Velikovski will certainly encourage them to do so, if only because he thinks that the world may well be destroyed by a cosmic collision within a few thousand years, as it probably will if his history is correct. In fact the book is equally a degradation of science and of religion.

The "journals" quoted on the dust cover of *Worlds in Collision* were the New York *Herald Tribune* and *This Week* magazine section, and neither of them was in favor of atomic warfare or of making Great Britain the base for such warfare. *Worlds in Collision* describes frightening natural events that took place in the past, but is very careful not to provoke any fear of repetitions of such events in the future.

I regarded the publication of *Worlds in Collision* as a

warning against atomic warfare. Disaster may come, not from another planetary collision, but from the handiwork of man himself, a victim of amnesia, in possession of thermonuclear weapons. The concluding paragraph to the Preface to *Worlds in Collision* reads:

> The years when *Ages in Chaos* and *Worlds in Collision* were written were years of a world catastrophe created by man—of war that was fought on land, on sea, and in the air. During that time man learned how to take apart a few of the bricks of which the universe is built—the atoms of uranium. If one day he should solve the problem of the fission and fusion of atoms of which the crust of the earth or its water and air are composed, he may perchance, by initiating a chain reaction, take this planet out of the struggle for survival among the members of the celestial sphere.

Haldane also implied in his review that the author of *Worlds in Collision* had deliberately left several clues to the effect that the book was planned as a hoax and that it might lead to world destruction.

This review, filled with misrepresentations that only an unreasoned reaction could produce, was followed by a thoroughly misleading reply to my rejoinder in *The New Statesman and Nation*, February 3, 1951.

Haldane, a biologist and philosopher, wished to be known as the embodied conscience of the scientific and philosophical worlds. England, his native land, he believed, was irreparably below all moral standards, and toward the end of his life, irrationally attracted by the esoteric, he left for India to die there.

Haldane's fury came out of his own irritation, caused in great measure by the impulses connected with inherited racial memories, while he himself believed in the righteousness of his cause. He felt the need to exorcise the spirit that possessed him, but instead exorcised my book. And he made dishonest statements, which one can understand as irrational and therefore excusable; finally he went off in search for a nirvana—and found none.

Not much different is the case of Eugene Rabinowitch, former editor of the *Bulletin of the Atomic Scientists,* a journal that was created to expiate the sin of the scientists who ate from the tree of knowledge of good and evil, and then built atomic bombs. Dr. Rabinowitch embraced the mission of becoming the conscience of the scientific community; the vision of doomsday was relentlessly before him. He, too, projected the fear of atomic disaster on *Worlds in Collision.* In 1964, when a series of "unexpected" confirmations renewed the interest in the book, he conducted a campaign against it, whereas the accumulating evidence required the opposite—a careful investigation by scientists of its tenets. He engaged H. Margolis, a journalist, to write on subjects in which both of them were complete ignoramuses (such as Hebrew and Egyptian philology), to deflate my handling of a certain text found in el-Arish carved on a *naos,* or stone shrine.[30]

These examples, and they could be multiplied, document the projection of fear of atomic disaster not toward its source in our mental heritage, but toward the *disclosure* of that source. It is a negative reaction, in Freud's nomenclature: a combination of not wishing to become aware of hidden springs, and an emotional reaction against that which may bring awareness of the cause of the mental disturbance.

[30] H. Margolis, "Velikovsky Rides Again," in *Bulletin of the Atomic Scientists* (April 1964).

A FIRMAMENT

The example of Darwin, a victim of amnesia with respect to experiences of his fieldwork, is not a unique case. It is more in the nature of a rule. The denial of terrifying experiences, or the suppression of awesome thoughts suggested by observations, can be witnessed again and again. Any one of us who chances to have a mishap that is more than he can live with in conscious memory is likely to deny the experience, or misinterpret it.

From the many cases at my disposal, I shall select the case of Loren Eiseley, anthropologist and historian of science, and, at the time he wrote the book from which I quote, provost of the University of Pennsylvania.

In 1960 he published *The Firmament of Time*. On the very first page one reads:

. . . scarcely two hundred years have passed since a few wary pioneers began to suspect that the earth might be older than the 4004 years B.C. assigned to it by the theologians. At all events, the sale of Velikovsky's *Worlds in Collision* a few years ago was a formidable indication that after the passage of two centuries of scientific endeavor, man in the mass was still enormously susceptible to the appeal of cataclysmic events, however badly sustained from the scientific point of view. It introduced to our modern generation, bored long since with the endless small accretions of scientific truth, the violence and catastrophism in world events which had so impressed our forefathers.

Eiseley's book was written to combat the reemergence of the discarded concept of catastrophic interruptions in history that was the teaching of the founders of the sciences of geology and paleontology in the early nineteenth century. But they, Murchison and Sedgwick and Buckland, were not among those who subscribed to the idea of Creation in the year 4004 before the present era: they had actually identified and named the Silurian and the Devonian and the Permian rocks and with them the periods so classified, the great divisions of the geological succession that antedated the emergence of man.

In *Earth in Upheaval* I quoted several authors who described the enigmatic and unquestionably catastrophic destruction of numerous animal species at the end of the Pleistocene, or Ice Age, at the beginning of the Neolithic period. I cited a paper that Eiseley published in 1943 when he was with the University of Kansas, quoting an observer of the awe-inspiring scene spread all over Alaska:

> . . . in certain regions of Alaska the bones of these extinct animals lie so thickly scattered that there can be no question of human handiwork involved. Though man was on the scene of the final perishing, his was not, then, the appetite nor the capacity for such giant slaughter.

Because of the wholesale and rapid extermination of fauna, Eiseley maintained, "it seems impossible to attribute the phenomenon to the unaided efforts of man."[31] In this great carnage are myriads of animals, limb torn from limb, in great heaps over tens of miles, mixed with splintered trees. It was not a mirage nor a phantasmagoria: other scientists described it, too. The animals are from all kinds of habitats, forms still existing and forms extinct, alike. The same phenomenon is repeated in numerous places of the North and South American continents. Eiseley wrote:

> We are not dealing with a single, isolated relic species but with a considerable variety of Pleistocene forms, all of

[31] Quoted by Eiseley, *American Antiquity*, 8, No. 3 (1943), p. 217.

which must be accorded, in the light of cultural evidence, an approximately similar time of extinction.[32]

In *Earth in Upheaval* I also quoted other authors of the same school of thought as Eiseley, and their clear statement that catastrophic events of continental, even global dimension took place. "At approximately the same time we witness a similar extinction of mammal faunas of Africa and Asia."[33] This is how I described the consensus concerning the great extinction:

These species are believed to have been destroyed "to the last specimen" in the closing Ice Age. Animals, strong and vigorous, suddenly died out without leaving a survivor. The end came, not in the course of the struggle for existence— with the survival of the fittest. Fit and unfit, and mostly fit, old and young, with sharp teeth, with strong muscles, with fleet legs, with plenty of food around, all perished.[34]

Eiseley wrote on this score that these facts:

. . . drive the biologist to despair as he surveys the extinction of so many species and genera in the closing Pleistocene.[35]

and again:

It seems odd that a fauna which had survived the great ice movement should die at its close. But die it did.[36]

He professed not to know the cause of extinction but he described it in catastrophic terms. He could only state that

[32] Ibid., p. 215.
[33] G. E. Pilgrim, *Geological Magazine* (London), 81, No. 1.
[34] Velikovsky, *Earth in Upheaval*, p. 228.
[35] Eiseley, *American Anthropologist*, 48 (1946), p. 54.
[36] Eiseley, *American Antiquity*, 8, No. 3 (1943), p. 211.

geological and climatic changes occurred at the same time as animals were destroyed to the last in many places, decimated in others.

The "despair" of the scientist turned into denial of catastrophes, a very interesting and well-authenticated psychological problem. Alexis Carrel, a biologist who was much interested in psychology, wrote in *Man, the Unknown* concerning this phenomenon of denial as it applies to scientists and the problems for which they do not know an answer:

> Certain matters are banished from the field of scientific research, and refused the right of making themselves known. Important facts may be completely ignored. Our mind has a natural tendency to reject the things that do not fit into the frame of the scientific or philosophical beliefs of our time. After all, scientists are only men. . . . They willingly believe that facts that cannot be explained by current theories do not exist.

Returning to Eiseley's *The Firmament of Time*, we read:

> Catastrophism, in essence, may be said to have died of common sense. As a modern historian, Charles Gillispie, has commented, "To imagine the Divine Craftsman as forever fiddling with His materials, forever so dissatisfied with one creation of rocks or animals that He wiped it out in order to try something else, was to invest Him with mankind's attributes instead of the other way about."

This argument against catastrophism does not sound persuasive or even remotely scientific; the catastrophists of the nineteenth century were operating with geological and paleontological evidence, not with theological argument. Eiseley followed the quote from Gillispie with the statement: "Slowly the accumulation of geological information began to lead back toward the pathway pursued earlier by James Hutton. . . ." And Charles Lyell, who was born in the year Hutton died, "saw no evidence of world-wide catastrophes. He observed, instead, local disconformities of strata, the rise and fall of coast lines, the slow upthrust of mountain systems."

But if Lyell (who relied mainly on observations of others) did not see such evidence, Eiseley himself saw it. How, then, does it come about that he lost sight of it, when he denied that such evidence exists?

It existed also in the days of Lyell, and it was as unambiguous as that which Eiseley a hundred years later observed and described.

As a psychoanalyst I returned many times to the problem of awakening the human conscious mind to the forgotten heritage of ages. The traumatic experiences that humans keep buried in oblivion possess enormous power over the destiny of nations. *If the human race is not made able to face its past, the traumatic experience that caused cultural amnesia will demand repetition—and since the atomic age began, humans have lived under the sword of Damocles.*

Chapter III

IN FEAR AND TREMBLING

PLANET GODS

The agitation and trepidation preceding global upheavals, the destruction and despair that accompanied them and the horror of possible repetition all caused a variety of reactions, at the base of which was the need to forget, but also the urge to emulate. Astrologers and stargazers, as well as sooth-sayers, divined; conquerors excelled in wanton and cruel devastation, invoking and imitating planetary models. Prophets and seers exhorted and priests propitiated. Astronomy became the dominant occupation of the sages of the past in Mexico, in Assyro–Babylonia and elsewhere—precisely because of the cataclysmic events that took place. Astrology interested itself chiefly in the relative positions of the planets and with their conjunctions. In the first century before the present era, the Greek historian Diodorus of Sicily, after recording that the Chaldeans asserted that planets change their velocities and periods of time, says: "These stars exert the greatest influence for both good and evil upon the nativity of men; and it is chiefly from the nature of these planets and the study of them that they know what is in store for mankind."[1]

[1] Diodorus, *The Library* by C. H. Oldfather (Loeb Classical Library, 1933), II. 31. 1.

Diodorus' statement is to some extent correct, because of the great changes the encounters with other planets brought upon mankind and everything else living on this planet. But from the truth of the Chaldeans' belief to the wrong conclusions was but a short distance. Since the planets at their different encounters caused flood, hurricane, conflagration, destruction of animals or appearance of new plants, man could easily conclude that the "influence" was the result of a special character of a planet, which therefore must be placated. Thus religion originated with the worship of the astral bodies. So did architecture, with the building of great temples—the Parthenon, built to honor Athene, and the temple of Zeus, of which a few large columns are still standing in Athens; the temples to Jupiter in Baalbek, and to Amon, who was Jupiter, in Karnak, and to various deities of the past, all of them astral gods. Engineering, too, developed as a result of the catastrophes, because the great pyramids in Egypt (the greatest engineering feat of the past) were—in my understanding—royal shelters against possible repetition of catastrophic events.

Organized warfare has its inspiration in the same terror. As the ancient Assyrian kings went to war, they compared the destructiveness of their acts to the devastations caused by the astral deities at the time of the upheavals.

Since many generations saw the pandemonium of an apparent theomachy, or battle of the planetary gods, it was but natural for people on Earth to take sides. To worship the entire pantheon simultaneously was illogical; but to worship a selected planetary deity or deities meant incurring the wrath of opposing deities. This dilemma was another reason for mental disbalance in man, and in nations.

THE FEAST OF LIGHT

Most of the religious rites and observances of all creeds have been derived from ancient mysteries that go back to the events of the past in which celestial gods—Saturn, Jupiter and other planetary bodies—participated and left indelible memories. As an example of this notion I shall try in this short section to convey something I understood and wrote about, although in incomplete form, more than three decades ago. I considered not mentioning these events here at all, because, told with such brevity, the story may sound fantastic. But on the chance that I will not get around to presenting the story of Saturn and Jupiter in books (*Saturn and the Flood, Jupiter of the Thunderbolt*),* I add here a few guideposts.

Whoever should study ancient cults and mysteries, Osirian, Dionysian, Orphic, Eleusian, and others, would find that they came into being to symbolize, to repeat, to imitate the events of the past and the fates of planetary gods. I shall not enter here this wide domain, leaving the theme to those willing and able to master the subject. But I shall say a little about one of these cults, the Osirian. This cult and the mysteries connected with it dominated the Egyptian religion as nothing else. The myth of Osiris "is too remarkable and occurs in too many divergent forms not to contain a considerable element of historic truth," according to Alan Gardiner.[2] But what historical truth is it? Could it be that of "an ancient king upon whose tragic death the entire legend hinged"? But of such a king "not a trace has been found be-

* Velikovsky's writings on these subjects are being prepared for future publication.

[2] Alan Gardiner, *Egypt of the Pharaohs* (Oxford University Press, 1961), p. 424.

fore the time of the Pyramid Texts," and in these texts Osiris
is spoken of without end. There he appears as a dead god, or
king and judge of the dead. Alternatively "he is presented
to us as the vegetation which perishes in the flood-water
mysteriously issuing from himself. . . ."[3] He is also associated with brilliant light; he was dismembered; Isis, his
spouse, went in search of his dispersed members; Isis gave
birth to Horus whom she conceived from Osiris.

James G. Frazer, the collector of folklore, came to regard
Osiris as the vegetation god; likewise he saw in Tammuz,
the Babylonian Osiris, a vegetation god. Carried away by
this concept, he wrote *The Golden Bough,* built around the
idea of the vegetation god who dies and is resurrected the
next year.

Of Tammuz it is also narrated that he was associated with
brilliant light, with flood, with descent into the netherworld,
visited there by Ishtar, his spouse. Osiris'—or Tammuz'—
death, then his resurrection, or his being found in the far
reaches but no longer brilliant, were the theme of what was
not just one of the mysteries, but the great and paramount
cult. The death of Tammuz was lamented; so was the death
of Osiris. As late as the end of the Judean Kingdom, in the
time of Jeremiah and Ezekiel, in the Hebrew month of Tammuz women of Judea cried for the god Tammuz (Ezekiel
8:14) and a fasting was held; the same took place in the entire area of the ancient East.

After a life of studying Egyptian history and religion,
Gardiner, the leading scholar in these fields, confessed that
he remained unaware of whom Osiris represents or me-
morializes.

Osiris in my understanding was not a king but the planet
Saturn, Cronos of the Greeks, Tammuz of the Babylonians.
The age of Cronos was the Golden Age; it came to its end in

---

[3] Ibid., p. 426.

the universal Deluge. The seventeenth day of Tammuz (June–July) was the first day of lamentations that continued for weeks. The seventeenth day of the month also plays a conspicuous role in the story of the Deluge.

The "light of seven days" of which Isaiah speaks (Isaiah 30:26) refers, in my understanding, to the "seven days" just before the beginning of the Deluge (Genesis 7:4). The whole world was brilliantly lit: Saturn flared as a nova. Its light was unbearably bright ("like that of a hundred suns" in rabbinical lore). Saturn or Cronos, Tammuz, Osiris—all were brilliant gods before being extinguished. A universal deluge followed in which not only the Earth, but the entire solar system was bathed. Water on Earth increased several fold. It appears that the Atlantic, the younger ocean, then first came into being; it was called the Sea of Cronos. On the Earth many forms of life perished in the Deluge, and many new genera of animal and plant life came into being in mutations on a scale unprecedented in human memory. This made Osiris or Tammuz or Cronos appear as a god of vegetation.

Jupiter collected much of the dispersed material and, rotating ever more swiftly, underwent fission.

Saturn, prominent in the sky—possibly even the star around which the Earth revolved—became invisible until once again found, now with rings around it. The Greek legend made Jupiter a son of Saturn, in the sense that Jupiter took over the dominion of the sky. It was also Jupiter who put Saturn in bonds. But in the Egyptian way of viewing the celestial drama, it was Isis (Jupiter), the spouse of Osiris (Saturn) who wrapped him in swaths, the way the deceased are dressed for their journey to the world of the dead, over which Osiris reigns.

The feast of light in memory of Saturn was observed by

the Romans as the Saturnalia at the end of December. The observance of this festival was taken over by the Jewish Hanukkah and then by the festival of Christmas. The observance of festivals of light was universal, because the Deluge had been a universal experience.

FIRST CENTURY: VISIONS OF APOCALYPSE

In the middle of the fifteenth century before the present era the planet Earth passed through one of the greatest disasters ever and was scorched by fire and swept by hurricanes and huge tides. Seven hundred years later, in the days of Amos, Hosea, Joel and Isaiah, a new series of global upheavals—one disaster following another at short intervals—took place: the peoples of the Earth staggered at repeated close approaches of another *aster*. These two periods are described in *Worlds in Collision*. In the series of disasters between −776 and −687 the Earth, though moved from its axis and orbit, fared better than seven hundred years earlier.

When another stretch of seven hundred years had passed, in the first century before the present era, a terror reawakened in the consciousness of the peoples and manifested itself in conceptions and expectations which betray their source. The end of the world was feared, and in the first century this anticipation of the end of the world grew immensely. Teachings about the last days, or the new world to come, were an expression of ideas engendered by experiences in the past. From the time of the Dead Sea scrolls and of the brilliant comet that appeared in daylight for months following the violent death of Caesar, through the days of Jesus of Nazareth and of the Emperor Nero, of the Sibylline oracular writings, the Book of Revelation and the fall of Jerusalem, terror gripped the human race.

In the first century before the present era Lucretius, traditionally the prophet of doom, wrote about the catastrophes and their terror: "The mighty and complex system of the universe, upheld through many years, shall crash into ruins," he predicted. "Yet I do not forget how novel and strange it strikes the mind that destruction awaits the heavens and the earth. . . . My words will perhaps win credit by plain facts, and within some short time you will see the worlds in commotion and the universe convulsed with shocks. . . . the universe can collapse, borne down with a frightful-sounding crash." He recalled the earlier destructions witnessed by mankind, and the recentness of the present creation. Since it is known that "the generations of men have perished in scorching heat, or that their cities have been cast down in some great upheaval of the world, or that after incessant rains rivers have issued out to sweep over the earth and overwhelm their towns" it is also evident "that destruction will come to earth and sky." For there are not "bodies lacking that can perchance gather out of the infinite and overwhelm this sum of things in a violent hurricane or bring in any other disaster or danger." And he vividly depicted the precariousness of the present harmony: "The door of death is therefore not closed for the heavens, nor for the sun and earth and the deep waters of the sea, but stands open and awaits them with vast and hideous maw." For did it not happen once before that fire won out over the other elements and brought the world to the brink of destruction "when far from his course the furious might of the sun's horses whirled Phaethon throughout the sky and over all the earth. But the almighty father [Zeus], stirred then with fierce anger, crashed down ambitious Phaethon from his car to the earth with a sudden thunderbolt, and the sun, meeting his fall, caught up from him the everlasting lamp of the world, and bringing back the scattered horses, yoked them in trembling, and then guiding them on their proper path, restored all again."[4]

At the beginning of the present era Seneca wrote about the fate of the human race: "There will one day come an end to all human life and interests. The elements of the earth must all be dissolved or utterly destroyed. . . . the rock will everywhere gape in fissures, and the fresh supplies of water will leap down into the gulfs, and unite in forming one great sea. . . . A single day will see the burial of all mankind. All that the long forebearance has produced, all that is famous and all that is beautiful, great thrones, great nations, all will descend into one abyss, will be overthrown in one hour."

When the appointed day comes, many causes will conspire to destroy the present order—"nor will such upheaval come without the shaking of the entire world" (*neque enim sine concussione mundi tanta mutatio est*).[5]

The *Sibylline Oracles,* which originated in the same period, occupied themselves mainly with the expected catastrophe. The day would come when "God, Whose dwelling is in the sky, shall roll up the heaven as a book is rolled, and the whole firmament in its varied forms shall fall on the divine earth and on the sea; and then shall flow a ceaseless cataract of raging fire and shall burn land and sea, and the firmament of heaven and the stars and creation itself it shall cast into one molten mass and clean dissolve. Then no more shall there be luminaries, twinkling orbs, no night, no dawn . . . no spring, no summer, no winter, no autumn." A comet would presage the end: "In the west a star shall shine, which they call a comet, a messenger to men of the sword, famine and death." Entire cities would disappear in chasms

[4] Lucretius, *De Rerum Natura,* translated by W. Rouse (London, 1924), Bk. V., 95 f., 338 f., 395 f.

[5] Seneca, *Naturales Quaestiones,* translated by J. Clarke (London, 1910), III. 28, 29.

opened up in the earth or be consumed by fire falling from heaven.[6]

In the apocryphal *Book of Enoch* it is said that in the final days "the years shall be shortened, and the moon shall alter her order and not appear in her time. . . . And in those days the sun shall rise in the evening, and his great chariot shall journey to the west, causing distress, and shall shine more brightly than accords with the order of light. And many chiefs of the stars shall transgress the order [prescribed] and these shall alter their orbits and tasks and not appear at the seasons prescribed for them." Then Enoch saw a vision: ". . . the heaven collapsed and was borne off and fell to the earth. And when it fell to the earth I saw how the earth was swallowed up in a great abyss, and mountains were suspended on mountains, and hills sank down on hills, and high trees were rent from their stems, and hurled down and sunk in the abyss."[7]

Similarly wrote the apostle Peter: "But the heavens and the earth, which are now . . . reserved unto fire against the day of judgement and perdition. . . . But the day of the Lord will come as a thief in the night . . . the heavens shall pass away with a great noise, and the elements shall melt with fervent heat, the earth also and the works that are therein shall be burned up."

Jesus prophesied the end of the world in his days, and when it did not come and he died on the cross he was expected to return in the days of the apostles. And why were they "looking for and hasting unto the coming of the day of God, wherein the heavens being on fire shall be dissolved and the elements shall melt with fervent heat? Nevertheless we, according to his promise, look for new heavens and a

[6] *The Sibylline Oracles*, translated by Lanchester in R. H. Charles, ed., *Apocrypha and Pseudepigrapha of the Old Testament* (London, 1913), III, pp. 80 f., 334, 341.

[7] *Book of Enoch* (Ethiopian) 80:2–6.

new earth. . . .";[8] the "new heavens" is a sky with the position of constellations changed and with the Sun and the Moon traveling on changed paths; and the "new earth" has its poles reversed and climate changed, with new outlines of land and the expanse of the sea, with old mountains brought low and new mountains arising where plains had been. But the Son of Man who promised to come to judge the Earth tarried in coming.

Several decades passed. *The Apocalypse,* or *Book of Revelation,* the last in the canon of the New Testament, is a vision of a mystic named John while on the island of Patmos in the Aegean Sea. ". . . and there fell a great star from heaven. . . . and the third part of the sun was smitten, and the third part of the moon, and the third part of the stars. . . .

". . . Woe, woe, woe to the inhabiters of the earth. . . ."[9]

The phantasmagoria goes on; one frightful vision is supplanted by the next, even more frightful: a dragon appears in the sky, and another star falls, and a bottomless pit opens. Beasts of horror march in a procession of awe.

The fearful sufferings of the whole century before Jerusalem became *capta* in the claws of the Roman eagle, and the next century of broken hopes and disillusionment vexed many a soul with dread expectation of the end of the world —when evil would perish after the good and the true that had perished already.

It was a time when misery mounted over the power of men to endure it. The anguish of disturbed minds produced dreadful pictures of persecution, visions of grotesque beasts and apocalyptic distortions. In these visions a heritage of an archaic impression took the form of revelation.

Since the advent of early Christianity, the terrifying

[8] II Peter 3:7–12. Cf. I. Chaine, "*Cosmogonie aquatique et conflagration finale d'après la secunda Petri,*" *Revue Biblique,* 46 (1937), p. 207 f.
[9] Revelation 8:10–13.

scenes of the past have been moved into the future, to the days of the Second Coming, and made the lot of the sinners. But it was the unresolved submerged content from the *past* that really weighed heavily on the soul of every human being.

THE SEVENTH CENTURY AND THE DARK AGES

In the seventh century—the Dark Middle Age in Europe— the embers of long-extinguished fires suddenly blew hot in Arabia. An illiterate camel driver, who till then had worshipped the planet Venus,[10] felt in himself the spirit of the Lord's messenger, and his orations—the suras of the Koran— already in the next generation were carried by the sword of conquest to Morocco and to India. Of ancient times Mohammed (570?–632) knew only what he heard at random at the gates of the rabbinical schools of Medina, and this was confused in his mind—Miriam, sister of Moses, was for him the same as Mary, mother of Jesus,[11] and Jesus the same as Joshua, son of Nun, who carried on the conquest of Canaan. Haman, the Persian vizier, became a vizier of the Pharaoh of the Exodus.[12] But his message was of mountains moving and of nature revolting, and of life extinguishing for unbelievers when moral laws are broken down:

> They [the unbelievers] think the Day of Judgement is far off: but We see it near at hand.
> Are they waiting for the Hour of Doom to overtake them unawares? Its portents have already come.
> The Hour of Doom is drawing near.
> On that day the heaven will shake and reel, and the

[10] Al Kalbi. See Philip Hitti, *History of the Arabs* (Princeton, 1937), p. 99.
[11] *The Koran*, Chapter 19, translated by N. J. Dawood (London, 1956).
[12] Ibid., Chapters 29, 40.

mountains crumble and cease to be. . . . On that day the earth will be rent asunder and they shall rush from it in haste.

Wait for the day when the sky will pour down blinding smoke, enveloping all men: a dreadful scourge.

When earth with all its mountains is raised high and with one mighty crash is scattered in the dust—on that day the Dread Event will come to pass. Frail and tottering the sky will be rent asunder. . . .

When the sun ceases to shine; when the stars fall down and mountains are blown away . . . when the seas are set alight . . . and the heaven is stripped bare. . . .[13]

The change in the places of the stars, moving away together with the firmament, the disturbances in the Sun, the change in the geological structure of the Earth, the boiling and disappearance of the sea—all are images of the past.

MID-FOURTEENTH CENTURY: A PERIODICITY OF FRENZY

Once more seven hundred years passed, and in the fourteenth century the human race again expected doomsday. I reproduce a description of the calamities that took place and the terror they caused:[14]

"The middle of the fourteenth century was a period of extraordinary terror and disaster to Europe. Numerous portents, which sadly frightened the people, were followed by a pestilence which threatened to turn the continent into an unpeopled wilderness. For year after year there were signs in the sky, on the earth, in the air, all indicative, as men thought, of some terrible coming event. In 1337 a great

[13] Ibid., Chapters 70, 47, 57, 50, 44, 69, 81, respectively.
[14] Charles Morris, *Historical Tales: The Romance of Reality* (Lippincott, 1893), p. 162 f.

comet appeared in the heavens, its far-extending tail sowing deep dread in the minds of the ignorant masses. During the three succeeding years the land was visited by enormous flying armies of locusts, which descended in myriads upon the fields, and left the shadow of famine in their track. In 1348 came an earthquake of such frightful violence that many men deemed the end of the world to be presaged. Its devastations were widely spread. Cyprus, Greece, and Italy were terribly visited, and [the seismic tremor] extended through the Alpine valleys. . . . Mountains sank into the earth. . . . The air grew thick and stifling. There were dense and frightful fogs. Wine fermented in the casks. Fiery meteors appeared in the skies. A gigantic pillar of flame was seen by hundreds descending upon the roof of the pope's palace at Avignon. In 1356 came another earthquake, which destroyed almost the whole of Basel. What with famine, flood, fog, locust swarms, earthquakes, and the like, it is not surprising that many men deemed the cup of the world's sins to be full, and the end of the kingdom of man to be at hand.

"An event followed that seemed to confirm this belief. A pestilence broke out of such frightful virulence that it appeared indeed as if man was to be swept from the earth. Men died in hundreds, in thousands, in myriads, until in places there were scarcely enough living to bury the dead, and these so maddened with fright that dwellings, villages, towns, were deserted by all who were able to flee, the dying and the dead being left their sole inhabitants. It was the pestilence called the 'Black Death,' the most terrible visitation that Europe has ever known.

"This deadly disease came from Asia. It is said to have originated in China, spreading over the great continent westwardly, and descending in all its destructive virulence upon Europe, which continent it swept as with the venom of destruction. The disease appears to have been a very malig-

nant type of what is known as the plague, a form of pestilence which has several times returned, though never with
such virulence as on that occasion. . . . Villages and towns
were in many places utterly deserted, no living things being
left. . . .

"London lost one hundred thousand of its population; in
all England a number estimated at from one-third to one-
half of the entire population (then probably numbering
from three to five millions) were swept into the grave. If we
take Europe as a whole, it is believed that fully a fourth of
its inhabitants were carried away by this terrible scourge.
For two years the pestilence raged, 1348 and 1349. It broke
out again in 1361–62, and once more in 1369.

"The mortality caused by the plague was only one of its
disturbing consequences. The bonds of society were loos-
ened; natural affection seemed to vanish; friend deserted
friend, mothers even fled from their children; demoraliza-
tion showed itself in many instances in reckless debauchery.
An interesting example remains to us in Boccaccio's *Decam-
eron*, whose stories were told by a group of pleasure-lovers
who had fled from plague-stricken Florence.

"In many localities the hatred of the Jews by the people
led to frightful excesses of persecution against them, they
being accused by their enemies of poisoning the wells. From
Berne, where the city councils gave orders for the massacre,
it spread over the whole of Switzerland and Germany, many
thousands being murdered. . . ."

The religious excitement of the time gave vitality to the
sect of the Flagellants:

"The members of this sect, seeing no hope of relief from
human action, turned to God as their only refuge, and
deemed it necessary to propitiate the Deity by extraordinary
sacrifices and self-tortures. The flame of fanaticism, once
started, spread rapidly and widely. Hundreds of men, and

even boys, marched in companies through the roads and streets, carrying heavy torches, scourging their naked shoulders with knotted whips, which were often loaded with lead or iron, singing penitential hymns, parading in bands which bore banners and were distinguished by white hats with red crosses.

"Women as well as men took part in these fanatical exercises, marching about half-naked, whipping each other frightfully, flinging themselves on the earth in the public places of the towns. . . . Entering the churches, they would prostrate themselves on the pavement, with their arms extended in the form of a cross. . . .

". . . The day of judgement, they declared, was at hand. . . . They preached, confessed, and forgave sins, declared that the blood shed in their flagellations had a share with the blood of Christ in atoning for sin, that their penances were a substitute for the sacraments of the church, and that the absolution granted by the clergy was of no avail. They taught that all men were brothers and equal in the sight of God, and upbraided the priests for their pride and luxury.

". . . Some of them even pretended to be the Messiah, one of these being burnt as a heretic at Erfurt. . . ."

The portents in the sky and the pestilence that followed were enough to cause the frenzied expectation of doomsday: there was no need for a hidden cause for such a reaction; nevertheless, the repetition—now for the fourth time, always at an interval of close to seven hundred years—of natural events startlingly remindful of the happenings in the mid-fifteenth century before the present era, in the days of the Exodus and the collapse of the Middle Kingdom in Egypt, could not but add to the human terror. Such portents could easily have been magnified in the eyes of the world's population because the psychic attitude was preconditioned; in such a state of mind, man was also more readily a prey to contagious diseases.

It may even appear that nature itself maintained a periodicity of frenzy as if further to frighten the frightened. In any case racial memory of the first two outbursts of berserk elements prepared the mind for seeing, in natural phenomena of the kind that may occur in almost any century, forebodings of the final disaster.

Elsewhere I have described a phenomenon to which I applied the term "psychic anaphylaxis." Anaphylaxis is a medical term for an increased reaction to a second application of an irritant. Psychic anaphylaxis I called:

> . . . That phenomenon in the psychic life of man which, like its biological namesake, is characterized by a special sensitivity to an agent which has at one time happened to act on the individual, and which when again experienced causes a second reaction far exceeding the first in intensity. It is evident that the changes (in the body or mind) must have been far-reaching at the time they were first produced by the initial agent. However, the *latent* sensitivity they produced led to explosive acts only later through the action of a similar agent.[15]

An analogous process, affecting mankind as a whole on a time scale of centuries, may have intensified the terror that marked the first century before this era and the seventh and fourteenth centuries of this era. If we project this periodicity of frenzy, occurring at intervals of approximately seven hundred years, into the future, will the twenty-first century mark another epoch of terror and frenzy? And since the period of seven hundred years is only approximate, could the next explosion occur even earlier? Not only will the seven-

[15] Velikovsky, "Psychic Anaphylaxis and Somatic Determination of the Affects," *The British Journal of Medical Psychology*, 17, Part I (1937), p. 98.

hundred-year cycle for the first time coincide with the "millennial" time ("bimillennial," actually), but the human race now has in its hands such awesome means of destruction that unless it comes to understand its unconscious urge to relive the most terrifying experiences of its past, it may stray dangerously close to the precipice, risking near-self-destruction, and possibly biological degeneration as well.

"THERE'S NO HIDING PLACE
DOWN THERE"

In the summer of 1971 I spent some time in the Swiss Alps and made the acquaintance of St. Clair Drake, a professor of anthropology and sociology at Stanford University. He heard me lecturing and came to share with me what he, himself a West Indies black, had learned of eschatological beliefs among various ethnic and religious groups. After I listened to his animated narration I asked him to write down something of it. He did so, and with his permission I present here a few extracts from his already concise script.

"I am impressed by the extent to which conscious preoccupation with catastrophes—past and present—is characteristic of the adherents of some religious groups, and the two related facts that:

a. catastrophe is invested with 'hope,' being seen dialectically as a *necessary prelude* to an era more rewarding than the present one being experienced.

b. the personality types who hold this view, in certain groups, are not sadists (in action at least) or active participants in the generation of human catastrophe, but tend, rather, to be pacifist in orientation.

"I have had personal experience with, and studied, three such groups: (a) the more unsophisticated Afro-Americans (American 'Negroes'); (b) Jehovah's Witnesses; (c) Seventh-Day Adventists.

"I have discerned among Africans and Afro-Americans outside of, or who have rejected, the Judaeo–Christian tradition, the phenomenon of what I call 'The Samson Complex' —the passionate desire to *create* the catastrophe that will destroy both them and their oppressors.

"The Christian religious 'cult' among the more unsophisticated Afro-Americans has a strong stress in the belief that God destroys specific civilizations or peoples occasionally both by natural catastrophe (e.g., Sodom and Gomorrah) and by the use of human conflicts: and that there will be future catastrophes and a great culminating catastrophe at 'the end of the world.' The book of Revelation describes how it will occur; prophecies in Matthew made by Jesus after entering Jerusalem on Palm Sunday (first day of Passover week) also referred to it graphically. When it comes, the 'righteous' will be 'saved'—either miraculously and/or by being resurrected after their death. *A thousand years of peace and prosperity will ensue on a renewed earth*—the Millennium. This apocalyptic eschatology was shared with white fundamentalist believers.

"Concurrently with the preaching of such ideas by 'exhorters' a beautiful religious folk-music grew up—the 'spirituals' that express them. Here are a few examples of the Catastrophic Theme:

> (a) I ran to the rocks
>   to hide my face;
>   the rocks cried out,
>   'No hiding place'—
>   There's no hiding place
>   down there

(b) My Lord, what a morning!
     My Lord, what a morning!
     My Lord, what a morning!
     When the stars begin to fall

(c) I heard the sound of the coming
         of the Savior! (call)
       Fare thee well; Fare thee well (response)
     In that great gitting-up morning,
       Fare thee well; Fare thee well
     The stars shall fall from heaven,
       Fare thee well; Fare thee well. . . .
     Like wax the mountain melting—
       Fare thee well; etc.
     The seas they'll be a-boiling—
       Fare thee well, etc.
     The moon with blood a-dripping
       Fare thee well. . . .

"The leader sings many verses improvising all the cata-strophic details gleaned from Old and New Testament.

"All of the spirituals with catastrophic themes are eschatological, referring to the last final catastrophe, when the forces of Gog and Magog will meet in battle on the plains of Megiddo (Battle of Armageddon), and at the end of which the Messiah will appear (for the *second* time in Christian belief) and the New Jerusalem will come down out of Heaven 'adorned as a bride for her husband.' The book of Revelation is the major source for details. As I have heard them sung in worship services, these spirituals, sung with great fervor and beauty, express these emotions:

(a) awe and wonder at the unusual event which Je-hovah *can* and will use to bring judgment upon hu-man history

(b) fascination with the multiplicity of details—almost

enjoyment—like watching fireworks or, in modern days, a science fiction movie

(c) certitude that the 'saved' will survive it all, and a sense of relief over this fact

(d) anticipatory delight over enjoyment of the Millennial age. These are *not* spirituals, interestingly, but 'white' hymns incorporated into Negro services and sung with a distinctive 'Negro' rhythm and 'beat.'

"Jehovah's Witnesses, or Watchtower Movement"[16]

"Founded by Charles Taze Russell in the second half of the 19th century as one of many millennarian movements in the U. S. He predicted the 'end of the age' in 1914. His successor, Judge Rutherford (now dead), reworked the eschatological myth and set no date. Their magazine, *Awake*, and other publications are constantly interpreting what they call 'the signs of the times' to prove the 'end' is near. Their role is to 'Witness,' not participate in, the events that express God's wrath. For instance, wars are inevitable and necessary, but *they* are absolute pacifists and have been jailed in Hitler's Germany, U.S.S.R., U.S.A., etc. for refusing military service.

"Their publications indicate constant research in the fields of biology, geology, astronomy, physics, archaeology, etc. in a search for data on catastrophes, past and present, that indicate the end of one age and the beginning of another and that indicate we are living in 'the time of the end.' They are usually well-written articles that do not distort the factual data, but interpret in their frame of reference.

[16] Cf. St. Clair Drake, "Who Are Jehovah's Witnesses?" in *Christian Century* (1936), and the careful sociological study by Herbert H. Stroup, *The Jehovah's Witnesses* (Columbia University Press, 1945).

"The Seventh-Day Adventists.

"The one 19th Century American millennarian group that became institutionalized is now considered an 'orthodox' Protestant denomination. . . . Adventists believe that we are living at 'the time of the end,' but do not, as their founder did, set a date. They watch for 'signs of the times' diligently, and publish a well-edited magazine monthly called *Signs of the Times*. . . .

"The Adventists I knew were *not* looking forward to possible atomic annihilation of mankind with dread and horror, but with hopeful anticipation. They believe that this was the mechanism by which the new earth prophesied for the Millennial Age would come into being. The great release of radiation carried by fall-out all over the earth would change the genetic structure of flora and fauna (including man). Thus, lambs and lions could coexist happily and new men who would not want to take up arms against each other would be produced. Plants similar to those in Eden and mentioned in Revelation with 'leaves for the healing of the people' would exist. Adventists, being 'saved,' will survive the catastrophe and their transformed bodies will exist forever.

"Adventists, like Jehovah's Witnesses, feel that God, not they, should take human life. They will only serve in the ambulance corps in an army. They prize forbearance, gentleness, peace.

"Queries:

(1) How do we explain the fact that these groups do not seem to repress memories of past catastrophes?

(2) How do we explain their acceptance of, and even

welcoming of, disasters that will destroy millions, while in their *personal* lives they stress pacifist values?"

St. Clair Drake"

Chapter IV

POETS AND VISIONARIES

In later ages, in different places and cultures, there appears a visionary, a poet: suddenly, it is as if a door opens before him, with a light shining through, and he sees the past.

SHAKESPEARE, THREE GENERATIONS
AFTER COPERNICUS

On February 17, 1600, Giordano Bruno was burned at the stake in Rome. Before he died for his theological and astronomical heresies, he spent seven years in the prison of the Holy Inquisition in Venice and Rome. And before that he spent time in England trying to convince the great of the Elizabethan kingdom of the truth of the Copernican concept of the Sun, not Earth, in the center of the planetary system. This was before Galileo embraced the Copernican doctrine. Bruno, though a philosopher and not an astronomer, was in advance of his time: he saw in fixed stars other suns around which planets revolve, a view that made him an abhorrence to Kepler and Galileo. In England he did not succeed in promulgating the simple Copernican system—neither Shakespeare nor Bacon was swayed by his efforts, but steadfastly adhered to the Aristotelian system with the

Sun as one of the planets revolving like the rest around the Earth. Only William Gilbert, a physician and physicist, became convinced, whether through Bruno's efforts or his own, of the truth of the Copernican system and, through experiments, realized that the Earth is a huge magnet. He devised a solar system governed by magnetism in the motion of its parts. Bacon, the philosopher, is credited with introducing the principle of experiment and observation in scientific matters, instead of reliance on the word of authorities, usually ancient; but he was amused by Gilbert's experiments and decried them.

The fear of living on a moving planet must have been the basis for the rejection of the concept of a rotating Earth by Shakespeare, Bacon, and other great intellects of the age. Moving, Earth could come to a mishap; fixed, it is safely secured. In various of his works Shakespeare subscribed to the pre-Copernican system. In his innermost being, however, the poet must have known the reason this had to be palpably wrong: if Earth neither moves around the Sun nor rotates on its axis, then the spheres must be carried daily around the Earth at velocities for which nothing comparable was known on Earth.

> The heavens themselves, the planets, and this centre,
> Observe degree, priority, and place. . . .
> But when the planets
> In evil mixture, to disorder wander,
> What plagues, and what portents, what mutiny,
> What of raging of the sea, shaking of the earth,
> Commotion of the winds, frights, changes, horrors,
> Divert and crack, rend and deracinate. . . .
>
> (*Troilus and Cressida*, Act I)

Discord in nature is followed by a similar "oppugnancy" in human beings:

The bounded waters
Should lift their bosoms higher than the shores,
And make a sop of all this solid globe:
Strength should be lord of imbecility,
And the rude son should strike his father dead.

(*Troilus and Cressida*, Act I)

The racial memory rises from its submerged ward:

[King Lear] bids the wind blow the earth into the sea, or
swell the curled waters 'bove the main, that things might
change or cease . . . [and he asks that the] all-shaking
thunder, smite flat the thick rotundity o' th' world!

(*King Lear*, Act III)

The bard asks through the mouth of one of his characters:

Are not you moved, when all the sway of earth
Shakes like a thing unfirm?
. . . But never till to-night, never till now
Did I go through a tempest dropping fire.
Either there is a civil strife in heaven;
Or else the world, too saucy with the gods,
Incenses them to send destruction.

(*Julius Caesar*, Act I)

A phantasmagoria in Horatio's mind (*Hamlet*) reawakens
some ancient vision. The never-extinguished terror flamed
up when an unusually bright comet appeared soon after
Caesar's death, and the world awaited doomsday.

In the most high and palmy state of Rome,
A little ere the mightiest Julius fell,
The graves stood tenantless and the sheeted dead

Did squeak and gibber in the Roman streets:
As stars with trains of fire and dews of blood,
Disasters in the sun; and the moist star [the Moon]
Upon whose influence Neptune's empire stands
Was sick almost to doomsday with eclipse. . . .

(*Hamlet,* Act I)

To postpone doomsday, the Earth must be fixed, and in
the poet's expressed faith "the planets, and this centre, observe degree, priority, and place. . . ." This lullaby verse
was still heard three and a half centuries after Shakespeare.

THE SHADOW OF DEATH

Visions of the world on a collision course with a flaming
body growing ever larger and more menacing, or phantas-
magorias of celestial battle, all to some degree remindful of
the events witnessed by overawed humanity about to be
decimated—such visions reappeared in revelations of persons in ecstasy, in poetry of exalted lyricists, in dreams and
nightmares of ordinary men. The high waves rising pre-
cipitously and then crashing down; the all-leveling earth-
shocks; the fire rain descending from space; the flaming
mountains, bursting when swept by continent-invading
tides; the waves carrying the fragments to other mountain
barriers, themselves just sprung from the plains—these and
related visions are almost a repertoire of man's unconscious
mind. They rise occasionally to the level of the subconscious
and from there into the domain of poetical clairvoyance or,
as the case may be, into the nightmares of human beings
who awaken in a cold sweat.

Recognizing in so many instances an unmasked reflection
of events witnessed by overawed ancestors, events many of
which go back to the convulsion of nature thirty-four cen-

turies ago, I looked also for a similar reflection of the experiences of ancestors who, having survived the onslaught of cataclysmic events, were languishing in the semidarkness that enveloped the world. In *Worlds in Collision* I showed that "Shadow of Death" was the designation given to the conditions that followed the visitation of a wandering celestial body, in later centuries to become the planet Venus; and I quoted a neglected verse of Jeremiah (2:6) about the generation of the desert that groped in the Shadow of Death, and of which the Hebrew tradition persists that all of it was doomed to perish in the desert. Germanic mythology refers to it as *Goetterdaemmerung*.

Ancient Mexican traditions preserved in sacred services speak of the profound gloom that for a quarter of a century enveloped the Western continent, and I repeat here one summarizing quote by Charles Étienne Brasseur, the nineteenth-century explorer and archaeologist: "A vast night reigned over all the American land, of which tradition speaks unanimously: in a sense the sun no longer existed for this ruined world which was lighted up at intervals only by frightful conflagrations, revealing the full horror of their situation to the small number of human beings that escaped from these calamities."[1] In the section "Shadow of Death" (*Worlds in Collision*, pp. 126–34) I quoted traditions written in other ancient languages about the time the sky was shattered, the day became dark and stayed dark through decades, and Earth teemed with noxious creatures.

The generation of the Shadow of Death almost entirely succumbed, and its progeny emerged into the extended traumatic experience of a dying world—in Iceland the tradition is that in the somber Fimbul–Winter only one human pair survived. All this must have been stored in an un-

[1] Charles Étienne Brasseur, *Sources de l'histoire primitive du Mexique* (Maisonneuve et Cie., Paris, 1864), p. 47.

fathomably rich but condemned-to-oblivion storehouse of the human subconscious mind.

A friend, knowing of my search, sent me this poem of Lord Byron, *Darkness:*

> I had a dream, which was not all a dream.
> The bright sun was extinguished, and the stars
> Did wander darkling in the eternal space,
> Rayless, and pathless, and the icy Earth
> Swung blind and blackening in the moonless air;
> Morn came and went—and came, and brought no day,
> And men forgot their passions in the dread
> Of this their desolation; and all hearts
> Were chilled into a selfish prayer for light:
> And they did live by watchfires—and the thrones,
> The palaces of crowned kings—the huts,
> The habitations of all things which dwell,
> Were burnt for beacons; cities were consumed,
> And men were gathered round their blazing homes
> To look once more into each other's face;
> Happy were those who dwelt within the eye
> Of the volcanos, and their mountain-torch:
> A fearful hope was all the World contained;
> Forests were set on fire—but hour by hour
> They fell and faded—and the crackling trunks
> Extinguished with a crash—and all was black.
> The brows of men by the despairing light
> Wore an unearthly aspect, as by fits
> The flashes fell upon them; some lay down
> And hid their eyes and wept; and some did rest
> Their chins upon their clenched hands, and smiled;
> And others hurried to and fro, and fed
> Their funeral piles with fuel, and looked up
> With mad disquietude on the dull sky,
> The pall of a past World; and then again
> With curses cast them down upon the dust,

And gnashed their teeth and howled: the wild birds
    shrieked,
And, terrified, did flutter on the ground,
And flap their useless wings, the wildest brutes
Came tame and tremulous; and vipers crawled
And twined themselves among the multitude,
Hissing. . . .

. . . no Love was left;
All earth was but one thought—and that was Death,
Immediate and inglorious; and the pang
Of famine fed upon all entrails—men
Died, and their bones were tombless as their flesh;
The meagre by the meagre were devoured,

. . . The World was void . . .
Seasonless, herbless, treeless, manless, lifeless—
A lump of death—a chaos of hard clay. . . .

This fantasy of Byron was not born by fiat of the poet,
drawing his creative elixir out of a void, bringing into being
figures and situations invented by him and familiar to nobody else.

Details of the poem, like the reference to the volcanoes
blazing in the darkness, or creatures taking over the suddenly depopulated and impoverished world, or the flocks of
the terrified wild birds that fluttered on the ground while
the world was in pangs of hunger and despair, seem to echo
some ancient impressions. Byron showed no awareness of
the similarity in his poem to conditions at the time of the
Exodus and the wandering in the desert, when he spread
before his readers this picture of a world coming to an end.
But this is how the survivors of the initial shock—devastating as it was—must have viewed their existence in a world
expiring and not to be resurrected: was not some real happening buried in the human soul for over thirty centuries in

this grim picture of the flocks of birds fluttering helplessly
on the ground among famished wanderers in a land whirling
in ashes?

In *Earth in Upheaval* I tried to bring back to light the
effect of changed ecology on the animal kingdom, even
where man was not present to absorb the impressions. I
painted the scene as I saw it in the evidence presented by
stones and bones:

> . . . In changed surroundings, amid climatic vicissitudes,
> with pastures withered, with plants that had served as food
> or animals that had served as prey gone, these few followed
> the rest in a losing battle for existence, surrendering at last
> in the struggle for survival of a species.
>
> Burning forests, trespassing seas, erupting volcanoes, sub-
> merging lands took the major toll; impoverished fields and
> burned-down forests did not offer favorable conditions for
> frightened and solitary survivors, and claimed their own
> share in the work of extinction.

Lord Byron did not write an eschatological picture of a
dying world of the *future*, as he thought he did: he drew
from a common spring of all men, even of all the animal
kingdom.

NEVERMORE

Edgar Allan Poe wrote a short tale, "The Conversation of
Eiros and Charmion." Upon ending his earthly life, Eiros
has just arrived in the Beyond and is greeted there by Charmion: they knew each other when on Earth. Charmion, for a
number of years a denizen of the Land of Bliss ("Aidenn"),
says:

"I am burning with anxiety to hear the details of that stupendous event which threw you among us. Tell me of it . . .

of the world which has so fearfully perished. . . . When, coming out from among mankind, I passed into Night through the Grave—at that period, if I remember aright, the calamity which overwhelmed you was utterly unanticipated. But, indeed, I knew little of the speculative philosophy of the day."

Eiros replies:

"The individual calamity was, as you say, entirely unanticipated; but analogous misfortunes had been long a subject of discussion with astronomers. I need scarce tell you, my friend, that even when you left us, men had agreed to understand those passages in the most holy writings which speak of the final destruction of all things by fire, as having reference to the orb of the earth alone. But in regard to the immediate agency of the ruin, speculation had been at fault from that epoch in astronomical knowledge in which the comets were divested of the terrors of flame. The very moderate density of these bodies had been well established. They had been observed to pass among the satellites of Jupiter, without bringing about any sensible alteration either in the masses or in the orbits of these secondary planets. We had long regarded the wanderers as vapory creations of inconceivable tenuity, and as altogether incapable of doing injury to our substantial globe, even in the event of contact. But contact was not in any degree dreaded; for the elements of all the comets were accurately known. That among *them* we should look for the agency of the threatened fiery destruction had been for many years considered an inadmissible idea. But wonders and wild fancies had been, of late days, strangely rife among mankind; and although it was only with a few of the ignorant that actual apprehension prevailed, upon the announcement by astronomers of a *new* comet, yet this announcement was generally received with I know not what of agitation and mistrust.

"The elements of the strange orb were immediately calculated, and it was at once conceded by all observers, that its path, at perihelion, would bring it into very close proximity with the earth. There were two or three astronomers, of secondary note, who resolutely maintained that a contact was inevitable. I cannot very well express to you the effect of this intelligence upon the people. For a few short days they would not believe an assertion which their intellect, so long employed among worldly considerations, could not in any manner grasp. But the truth of a vitally important fact soon makes its way into the understanding of even the most stolid. Finally, all men saw that astronomical knowledge lied not, and they awaited the comet. Its approach was not, at first, seemingly rapid; nor was its appearance of very unusual character. It was of a dull red, and had little perceptible train. For seven or eight days we saw no material increase in its apparent diameter, and but a partial alteration in its color. Meanwhile the ordinary affairs of men were discarded, and all interests absorbed in a growing discussion, instituted by the philosophic, in respect to the cometary nature. Even the grossly ignorant aroused their sluggish capacities to such considerations. The learned *now* gave their intellect—their soul—to no such points as the allaying of fear, or to the sustenance of loved theory. They sought—they panted for right views. They groaned for perfected knowledge. *Truth* arose in the purity of her strength and exceeding majesty, and the wise bowed down and adored.

"That material injury to our globe or to its inhabitants would result from the apprehended contact, was an opinion which hourly lost ground among the wise; and the wise were now freely permitted to rule the reason and the fancy of the crowd. It was demonstrated, that the density of the comet's *nucleus* was far less than that of our rarest gas; and the harmless passage of a similar visitor among the satellites of Jupiter was a point strongly insisted upon, and which served greatly to allay terror. Theologists, with an ear-

nestness fear-enkindled, dwelt upon the biblical prophecies, and expounded them to the people with a directness
and simplicity of which no previous instance had been
known. That the final destruction of the earth must be
brought about by the agency of fire, was urged with a spirit
that enforced everywhere conviction; and that comets were
of no fiery nature (as all men now knew) was a truth which
relieved all, in a great measure, from the apprehension of
the great calamity foretold. It is noticeable that the popular
prejudices and vulgar errors in regard to pestilences and
wars—errors which were wont to prevail upon every appearance of a comet—were now altogether unknown. As if by
some sudden convulsive exertion, reason had at once hurled
superstition from her throne. The feeblest intellect had
derived vigor from excessive interest.

"What minor evils might arise from the contact were
points of elaborate question. The learned spoke of slight
geological disturbances, of probable alterations in climate,
and consequently in vegetation; of possible magnetic and
electric influences. Many held that no visible or perceptible
effect would in any manner be produced. While such discus-
sions were going on, their subject gradually approached,
growing larger in apparent diameter, and of a more brilliant
luster. Mankind grew paler as it came. All human operations
were suspended.

"There was an epoch in the course of the general sentiment when the comet had attained, at length, a size surpassing that of any previously recorded visitation. The people
now, dismissing any lingering hope that the astronomers
were wrong, experienced all the certainty of evil. The chi-
merical aspect of their terror was gone. The hearts of the
stoutest of our race beat violently within their bosoms. A
very few days sufficed, however, to merge even such feelings
in sentiments more unendurable. We could no longer apply
to the strange orb any *accustomed* thoughts. Its *historical*

attributes had disappeared. It oppressed us with a hideous *novelty* of emotion. We saw it not as an astronomical phenomenon in the heavens, but as an incubus upon our hearts, and a shadow upon our brains. It had taken, with inconceivable rapidity, the character of a gigantic mantle of rare flame, extending from horizon to horizon.

"Yet a day, and men breathed with greater freedom. It was clear that we were already within the influence of the comet; yet we lived. We even felt an unusual elasticity of frame and vivacity of mind. The exceeding tenuity of the object of our dread was apparent; for all heavenly objects were plainly visible through it. Meantime, our vegetation had perceptibly altered; and we gained faith, from this predicted circumstance, in the foresight of the wise. A wild luxuriance of foliage, utterly unknown before, burst out upon every vegetable thing.

"Yet another day—and the evil was not altogether upon us. It was now evident that its nucleus would first reach us. A wild change had come over all men; and the first sense of *pain* was the wild signal for general lamentation and horror. The first sense of pain lay in a rigorous constriction of the breast and lungs, and an insufferable dryness of the skin. It could not be denied that our atmosphere was radically affected; the conformation of this atmosphere and the possible modifications to which it might be subjected, were now the topics of discussion. The result of investigation sent an electric thrill of the intensest horror through the universal heart of man.

"Why need I paint, Charmion, the now disenchained frenzy of mankind? That tenuity in the comet which had previously inspired us with hope, was now the source of the bitterness of despair. In its impalpable gaseous character we clearly perceived the consummation of Fate. Meantime a day again passed, bearing away with it the last shadow of Hope. We gasped in the rapid modification of the air. The red blood bounded tumultuously through its strict channels. A furious delirium possessed all men; and, with arms rigidly outstretched toward the threatening heavens, they trembled and shrieked aloud. But the nucleus of the destroyer was now upon us: even here in Aidenn, I shudder while I speak. Let me be brief—brief as the ruin that overwhelmed. For a moment there was a wild lurid light alone, visiting and penetrating all things. Then—let us bow down, Charmion, before the excessive majesty of the great God!—then, there came a shouting and pervading sound, as if from the mouth itself of HIM; while the whole incumbent mass of ether in which we existed, burst at once into a species of intense flame, for whose surpassing brilliancy and all-fervid heat even the angels in the high Heaven of pure knowledge have no name. Thus ended all."

The description of a collision of the Earth with a wandering comet, found in Laplace, could not have served Poe as a sole model. Laplace limited his description to physical phenomena and consequences; Poe, however, to visual and auditory sensations, but mainly to the mental anguish of humanity in the face of the approaching terminal event. Certain facts are mentioned which could not have been deduced from the sum of scientific knowledge of Poe's time, almost three score years before the observations (1900) of the Dutch botanist, Hugo deVries, on the evening primrose, given to spontaneous but very rudimentary mutations.

Poe's astronomers' arguments must strike the reader who is aware of the debate of the 1950s (evoked not at the appearance of a comet but at the appearance of a book) as familiar: comets are bodies without substance; none was seen to disturb any of the Jovian satellites while passing through the system, and the like. Thus one might be tempted to claim a certain prescience in the poet, although a search in literature would show that astronomers of the time employed the very same arguments to alleviate fearful expectations at the approach of spectacular comets. This may rationally explain some of the elements of Poe's story, but not all of them.

The anguish set forth by Poe impresses as a heritage of an extinct generation, or, better, of extinct generations—a trust unrecognized but real and troubling deep inside, under the muffling layer of the conscious mind, the scientist's as well as the layman's. With poetic clairvoyance, Poe temporarily peeled off the muffling strata, and the agony was all there, with its horror welling up and ebbing in crescendo and diminuendo, finally blazing out in a brilliance known to modern man only since the atomic explosion in the desert of Los Alamos.

Poe sensed the hidden anxiety of our race when he looked on the dissolution of life on Earth as already having happened. The Land of Shades—our terrestrial existence—is left behind: *all is ended.* Nor does any record exist of what might have befallen the dwellers on other planets that dutifully roll around the Sun on regular, if changed, paths. Nothing reveals that those planets might have nurtured advanced life before the dissolution into elements spelled out a "Nevermore."

MIND AT THE END OF ITS TETHER

Jules Verne (1828–1905) was a new type of prophet—nothing of his compatriot Nostradamus who preceded him by three hundred years; nothing of mysticism—all frivolous fantasy of science fiction. He described some of the adventurous enterprises of our age; and in the case of man's travel

to the Moon, in an uncanny fashion, one hundred years before Apollo 11, he invented some details that became reality
in the 1969 mission. But when he reached the age of sixty
his spring dried up and his mantle was snatched by H. G.
Wells.

In *The Time Machine, The War of the Worlds* and *In the
Days of the Comet,* Wells mixed science fiction with social
fiction, and his exuberant optimism carried him and his
readers to think that man's limits were not even the sky. He
also composed his famous short history of the world and was
preeminent among those who, though atheists or anti-
clerics, saw man's future as bright and worth improving, and
life as a time for enjoyment. However, I am not knowl-
edgeable enough about Wells to discuss him as a philosopher. As a prophet of technological progress, though constantly brimming with optimism, he was not always up to
the fantastic advances that waited in store: in 1907, in an article on "Modes of Transportation in the 20th Century," he
asserted that aeronautics would never become a means of
mass transportation. The breakneck pace of discoveries and
inventions that made this century, when compared with the
last, appear as if from another world epoch, surpassed the
imagination of science fiction writers. But then in the first
week of August, 1945, mushroom clouds above two cities in
faraway islands were handwriting in the sky proclaiming the
apple from the tree of knowledge to be a fruit of Sodom.

Before that event came to be, a world frenzied in destruction for six years struggled over the Teutonic Millennium.
Wells sat in London, paying scant attention to the bombs
falling around, contemplating his by now numerous infirmi-
ties, and writing *Mind at the End of Its Tether*. The atomic
age had not yet arrived. But it must have been terror inherited from ancestors, never before breaking to the surface
in him, or else a vision of a pregnant future, an eschatology,
focused on the nearest future, that turned a lifelong

preacher of hedonism and pleasure into a seer of imminent doom.

"The writer," so he started, "finds very considerable reason for believing that, within a period to be estimated by weeks and months rather than by aeons, there has been a fundamental change in the conditions under which life, not simply human life, but all self-conscious existence, has been going on since its beginning. This is a very startling persuasion to find establishing itself in one's mind, and he puts forward his conclusions in the certainty that they will be entirely unacceptable to the ordinary rational man."

He continued, speaking of himself in the third person: "If his thinking has been sound, then this world is at the end of its tether. The end of everything we call life is close at hand and cannot be evaded. He is telling you the conclusions to which reality has driven his own mind, and he thinks you may be interested enough to consider them, but he is not attempting to impose them upon you. He will do his best to indicate why he has succumbed to so stupendous a proposition. . . . He writes under the urgency of a scientific training, which obliged him to clarify his mind and his words to the utmost limit of his capacity."

It cannot be said that in pages to follow Wells made anything that could be counted as a scientific argument, or presented proof from nature or history, or a secret of war making. It is not what it is claimed to be—it is a vision of a visionary, seeing the future or knowing the hidden past.

"It requires an immense and concentrated effort of realisation, demanding constant reminders and refreshment, on the part of a normal intelligence, to perceive that the cosmic movement of events is increasingly adverse to the mental make-up of our everyday life. It is a realization the writer finds extremely difficult to sustain. But while he holds it, the significance of Mind fades. The secular process loses its accustomed appearance of a mental order."

After explaining what he meant by the term "secular" as referring to eternity, Wells proceeds, always referring to himself as "he":

"The secular process, as he now sees it, is entirely at one with such non-mental rhythms as the accumulation of cristalline matter in a mineral vein or with the flight of a shower of meteors. The two processes have run parallel for what we call Eternity, and now abruptly they swing off at a tangent from one another—just as a comet at its perihelion hangs portentous in the heavens for a season and then rushes away for ages or forever. Man's mind accepted the secular process as rational and it could not do otherwise, because he was evolved as part and parcel of it."

But how is it that Wells brings in as metaphor a shower of meteors and a portentous comet in the sky? Is not the simile here more than a simile?

In all his doomsday oration, Wells not even once put suspicion on man and man's action. Nature changed its flow and life is sentenced to extinction.

"The reality glares coldly and harshly upon any of those who can wrench their minds from the comforting delusions of normalcy to face the unsparing question that has overwhelmed the writer. They discover a frightful queerness has come into life. Even quite unobservant people now are betraying, by fits and starts, a certain wonder, a shrinking and fugitive sense that something is happening so that life will never be *quite* the same again."

Wells turns to the reader and admonishes him: "Spread out and examine the pattern of events, and you will find yourself face to face with a new scheme of being, hitherto unimaginable by the human mind. This new cold glare mocks and dazzles the human intelligence, and yet, such is the obstinate vitality of the philosophical urge in minds of that insatiable quality, that they can still, under its cold urgency, seek some way out or round or through the impasse.

The writer is convinced that there is no way out or round or through the impasse. It is the end."

Wells soon returns to similes of which the true significance is most suspicious:

"Hitherto events had been held together by a certain logical consistency, as the heavenly bodies as we know them have been held together by the pull, the golden cord, of Gravitation. Now it is as if that cord had vanished and everything was driving anyhow to anywhere at a steadily increasing velocity.

"The limit to the orderly secular development of life had seemed to be a definitely fixed one, so that it was possible to sketch out the pattern of things to come. But that limit was reached and passed into a hitherto incredible chaos. . . .

"Events now follow one another in an entirely untrustworthy sequence. No one knows what tomorrow will bring forth, but no one but a modern scientific philosopher can accept this untrustworthiness fully. . . . He knows, but the multitude is not disposed to know and so it will never know."

Never? If the cosmos approaches chaos and the laws of nature are soon to be terminated, there could be no secret for any length of time. But in the meantime—

"In that invincible ignorance of the dull mass lies its immunity to all the obstinate questioning of the disgruntled mind.

"It need never know. The behaviour of the shoal in which it lives and moves and has its being will still for a brief season supply the wanted material for that appreciative, exulting, tragic, pitiful or derisive comment which constitutes art and literature. Mind may be near the end of its tether, and yet that everyday drama will go on because it is the normal make-up of life and there is nothing else to replace it.

"To a watcher in some remote entirely alien cosmos, if we may assume that impossibility, it might well seem that extinction is coming to man like a brutal thunderclap of *Halt!*

". . . We may be spinning more and more swiftly into the vortex of extinction, but we do not apprehend as much."

A veil of deep gloom had descended on the most ebullient of the writers of his generation. It was not a case of a religious believer losing his faith. H. G. Wells had been an atheist since youth. He did not see the end in the fashion of Michelangelo's Sistine fresco; nor did he see the extinction of man and with him all life as the supreme debacle of *homo sapiens* upon reaching the forbidden summit. Nature, together with all its laws, thought to be eternal, disbands itself.

"A harsh queerness is coming over things and rushes past what we have hitherto been wont to consider the definite limits of hard fact. Hard fact runs away from analysis and does not return. . . . The limit of size and space shrinks and continues to shrink inexorably. The swift diurnal return of that unrelenting pendulum, the new standard of reference, brings it home to our minds that hard fact is outpacing any standard hitherto accepted. We pass into the harsh glare of hitherto incredible novelty."

Three thousand million years of Organic Evolution (Wells capitalizes these words) are swiftly coming to the end and the finale is in sight. ". . . The divergence widens between what our fathers were wont to call the Order of Nature and this new harsh implacable hostility to our universe, our *all*."

But who is hostile if there is no God and no Devil? Wells looked for a definition, "cosmic process," "the Beyond," "the Unknown," "the Unknowable," and rejected them all because they carry "unsound implications." Unable to formulate anything better, Wells settled on the "Antagonist." It will bring an end to evolution and the "dust-carts of Time trundle that dust off to the incinerator. . . ."

Does not one hear in Wells's agonized words the echo of

the Sibylline Oracles: ". . . and then shall flow a ceaseless cataract of raging fire, and shall burn land and sea, and the firmament of heaven and the stars and creation itself it shall cast into one molten mass and clean dissolve. Then no more shall there be the luminaries' twinkling orbs, no night, no dawn, no constant days of care, no spring, no summer, no winter, no autumn."

As if continuing the Sibylline prophecy, Wells rises from his seat in benighted London alight with the beacons of conflagrations and says:

"Hitherto, recurrence has seemed a primary law of life. Night has followed day and day night. But in this strange new phase of existence into which our universe is passing, it becomes evident that *events no longer recur*. They go on and on to an impenetrable mystery, into a voiceless limitless darkness, against which this obstinate urgency of our dissatisfied minds may struggle, but will struggle only until it is altogether overcome.

"Our world of self-delusion admits none of that. It will perish amidst its evasions and fatuities.

". . . the door closes upon us for ever more. There is no way out or round or through."

Is this a war-sick mind speaking to us? But Wells has not referred to the raging war, to Dunkirk or Coventry, or to the human beings herded into camps of death: he utters his sentences as if not man but lifeless nature has become pitiless.

"Our universe is not merely bankrupt . . . it has not simply liquidated; it is going clean out of existence, leaving not a wreck behind. The attempt to trace a pattern of any sort is absolutely futile.

"This is acceptable to the philosophical mind when it is at its most philosophical, but for those who lack that steadying mental backbone, the vistas such ideas open are so uncongenial and so alarming, that they can do nothing but hate, repudiate, scoff at and persecute those who express them, and betake themselves to the comfort and control of such refuges of faith and reassurance as the subservient fear-haunted mind has contrived for itself and others throughout the ages."

I interrupt the quote to contemplate: inadvertently Wells has revealed that the great fear which took possession of him is as old in the human race as religion. It would only be expected that in the next sentence he would let surface the ancestral fear of a destroyer from cosmic places, for whom he had sought a name.

"Our doomed formicary is helpless as the implacable Antagonist kicks or tramples our world to pieces. Endure it or evade it; the end will be the same. . . ."

In the pandemonium of bombed London, to which Wells was outwardly indifferent, surfaced an ancient, even primeval horror.

A year later, the much-plagued planet having circled once on its orbit, a blinding flash and a mushroom "as the smoke of a furnace" inaugurated the Age of Terror.

Chapter V

THE AGE OF TERROR

"WHY WAR?"

After World War I and only a single year before Hitler took over the German Reich, Albert Einstein and Sigmund Freud exchanged letters on the theme: "Why War?" Two great men of the generation, whose ideas colored the thinking of the first half of this century and continue to do so, engaged in an inquiry, Einstein, the physicist and pacifist, asking Freud, twenty-three years his senior, whether the field of psychiatry and psychoanalysis knows a panacea against the slaughter of human beings organized in states, against a sanctioned destruction of human life.

"It would be of the greatest service to us all were you to present the problem of world peace in the light of your recent discoveries, for such a presentation might blaze the trail for new and fruitful modes of action."

Freud in his reply gave a melancholy prognosis. He visualized "no likelihood of our being able to suppress humanity's aggressive tendencies."[1] The rest of Freud's reply was nothing but an elaboration on this verdict.

Bryant Wedge, writing on "Psychiatry and International Affairs" thirty-five years later, years that saw World War II

[1] Freud, *Collected Papers* (1950), vol. 5.

with the Holocaust and the atomic bomb, and wars in Korea
and Indochina, had this to say:

"This reply [by Freud] failed to undermine Einstein's
hope that psychiatry, the profession most practically concerned with disorder and conflict within and between
human individuals, might help in the management of relations among nations. That hope is still with us but continues
to be disappointed. Psychiatry has failed to provide practi-
cal assistance in the management of international conflict,
though such conflict has become vastly more dangerous to
mankind since the time of Einstein's appeal." Not that there
was no effort made on the part of psychiatrists. "In 1935,
339 psychiatrists from thirty nations signed a manifesto on
war prevention" in which the signatories stated: "We psychiatrists declare that our science is sufficiently advanced
for us to distinguish between real, pretended, and unconscious motives, even in statesmen."[2]

Two years later, in the summer of 1937, a large congress
of psychologists convened in Paris.[3] Professor Claparède of
Geneva read the main address, "Hatred among the Nations," which contained pious hopes and expressions of faith
in human progress. The paper I read was the only other discussion of the same theme.[4] My view, derived at that time
from psychoanalytical thinking, saw in repressed homosexuality of entire nations the source of hatred and of lust for
doing bodily harm on a mass scale, of the massacres and the
triumphs of a race motivated by male homosexuality,
against and over an effeminate nation. Is not the lust of the
Turks carrying massacre to an Armenian village enhanced
by these diversities in subconscious national make-up? Is
not Germany, with its national emblem of an eagle with

2 *Science*, 157 (21 July 1967). Dr. Bryant Wedge was head of the Institute
for the Study of National Behavior, Princeton, N.J.

3 XIe Congrès International de Psychologie, Paris, 25–31 July 1937.

4 "Les Origines psychologiques de la haine des Nations."

talons spread for piercing the victim's flesh, a natural enemy
of France, with its maiden in a Phrygian cap, and, alternatively, a chanticleer, a noisy but little frightening, almost
amusing, substitute for a male?

I still believe that suppressed homosexuality has much to
do with aggression. In the series of conflicts between Israel
and the Arab states the latter were thoroughly and repeatedly trounced by the Jews whose image through centuries of
dispersion was that of a persecuted and violated nation.
Thus the long-cherished self-esteem of Arabs as a male race
suffered so greatly that no concessions on the part of Israel
would pacify them.

Of my projected book *The Masks of Homosexuality*, my
paper entitled "Tolstoy's Kreutzer Sonata and Unconscious
Homosexuality" was published in Freud's magazine *Imago;*[5]
the rest was left fallow through my having become cap-
tivated by the recognition that grew into the themes of
Worlds in Collision, Ages in Chaos and *Earth in Upheaval.*

World War II of course did not hold off, waiting for psychologists to find and expose the roots of the scourge known
as war. "The idea that 'wars begin in the minds of men' and
that 'it is in the minds of men that defenses of peace must be
constructed' is as old as the history of relations between organized societies."

Dr. Wedge continued to quote from the Einstein–Freud
exchange of 1932; and observing the futility of the efforts,
he asked: "Why has the scientific profession most concerned
with helping the individual with the troubles of his mind
failed to contribute to solving the most significant problem
in all human behavior? What could psychiatry contribute?"

Wedge assessed the impotence of psychiatric science to
cope with the problem, but himself came up with nothing

[5] *Imago, Zeitschrift für psychoanalytische Psychologie,* 23 (1937), pp.
363–70; reprinted in English, translated by Dr. J. V. Coleman, *The Psychoanalytical Review,* 24 (January 1937).

more promising than "studies of the personality characteristics of foreign leaders, of psychopolitical factors in
specific international conflicts, of interpretation of negotiat-
ing behavior and of improving effectiveness of communication among nations," etc. These are hardly more than
generalities in some instances and palliatives in others. But
before he submitted these, he made a true observation:

"Psychiatry is primarily concerned with individual human
beings. Only recently has the revolutionary concept of social
interdependence led psychiatry to broader concerns, those
of the community and the nation as these bear on the history of individuals. The orthodox limits of psychiatry do little to prepare the profession for the scientific consideration
of international affairs.

"Psychiatrists who become concerned with the international world quite correctly perceive that dynamic psychological factors are somehow operative in it. Here, however,
the scale of the problem is baffling. . . ."

THE RECURRENT SCOURGE

There exists a seventeen-year locust. What makes the insect swarm after this long period is not known; no terrestrial
or extraterrestrial cause is obvious.

There is a similar phenomenon in the human race. Should
we investigate the great wars of the last few centuries we
would observe a certain periodical regularity in the return
of these great paroxysms. (I leave it to others to determine
whether such patterns can be found also in periods prior to
the last few centuries.)

From 1700 to 1709 the armies of Charles XII of Sweden
engulfed a large portion of Europe in wars of conquest.
Charles subdued Denmark, most of Germany, Poland, the
Baltic countries, and invaded the Ukraine. There, in the

heart of the country, near Poltava, far from his own land, he suffered defeat at the hands of Peter the Great.

At the same time Charles XII warred in eastern Europe, western Europe was the scene of a war (1701–14) in which France under Louis XIV, Spain and Bavaria were engaged against England, Holland, Austria, several German states and Portugal, with Savoy repeatedly changing sides. This "War of the Spanish Succession" was carried on along the Rhine and the Danube, in Flanders, Italy and Spain and on the seas; it resulted, among other things, in France's ceding Newfoundland and Nova Scotia to England, in Spain's ceding Gibraltar and Minorca and Portugal's asserting itself in Brazil.

A little more than a century later, actually 104 years after the outbreak of these hostilities, Napoleon made his onslaught on the combined forces of Prussia, Austria and Russia at Austerlitz (1805). He subdued most of Europe and fought deep into Russia in 1812, where he was defeated. He lost again at the Battle of the Nations (1813), and he fought a final battle at Waterloo (1815).

Again, a little over one hundred years later, the world was once more in flames. Germany under Wilhelm II led Austria–Hungary and Turkey against England, France and Russia. World War I engulfed many nations in Europe and in faraway parts of the world on an unprecedented scale. It continued from 1914 to 1918. There is an unmistakable pattern in this recurrence of events repeated after approximately 104 years.

But also halfway between these wars were wars of continental dimensions, so that the real pattern has fifty-two years from the beginning of one great explosion to the beginning of the next. In the eighteenth century it was the Seven Years' War (1756–63), the worldwide struggle of Austria, Russia, France and their allies against Prussia and England that gave England the decisive advantage over France in North America and India and the West Indies, and made Prussia the great opponent of Austria.

In the nineteenth century it was the Civil War (1861–65) in America during which hundreds of thousands of people were killed in one of the greatest slaughters in military history.

The last great paroxysm erupted at the half point of the regular fifty-two-year period: whereas World War I started in August 1914, World War II started in September 1939 but came to full expansion in 1940; it continued for six years, enveloping again the five continents. In the past the curve had a great rising wave every fifty-two years; in this century the great wave rose also at the half point of the period, or advanced by half a period.

A scrutiny of a graph of the major armed conflicts would reveal a short rise before and after each peak, these foothills denoting conflicts of minor magnitude or of confined character. Thus the Civil War was preceded by the Crimean War and followed by the Prussian exploits against Austria, Denmark and France. The First World War was preceded by the Balkan wars and followed by the civil war in Russia. World War II was preceded by the exploits of Mussolini against Ethiopia (as well as by the Spanish civil war and the war between Japan and China) and followed by the Korean War.

Following this pattern, a new great explosion of hostilities among nations was due in about 1966; the world entered into a state of tension and arms race and also of localized wars, in Vietnam and the Middle East. The atomic weapons developed since the end of World War II acted as a deterrent.*

---

* If there is sufficient flexibility in such cycles that a major explosion can be advanced by half a cycle (as with World War II) or that a major explosion that seems due can be deterred (as with 1966), then perhaps we should

If there is in the human race an urge for destruction and self-annihilation that comes to the fore at intervals of fifty-two and possibly also of twenty-six years (the span from the midpoint of World War I to the midpoint of World War II), then instead of political and economic factors, psychological or even biological factors must be thought of as fuses igniting outbursts in human masses. A state of irritability is a precondition for the "patriotic" intransigence that leads to great uncontrollable conflicts with trespass and maiming and killing. With the human race merging into great communities divided into camps, the local, "tribal" periods of conflict are themselves being merged into the sudden common explosions on a continental and, now in this century, a global scale.

The repetition of great conflicts, spaced at fifty-two-year periods and threatening also at half periods, must be considered as another natural phenomenon, like the swarming of locusts at seventeen-year periods (it could be noted in passing that the latter is about a third part of fifty-two, though the periods may have no relation to one another). The phenomenon of mass hysteria on a global scale must be understood and its roots must be searched and extracted.

The fact that two enormous natural cataclysms took place thirty-four centuries ago at this very interval of fifty-two years must be recalled, and if not affirmed as the biologically engendering cause of such periodical mass hysterias, then still suspected and investigated. The very suspicion and inquiry may themselves have healing effects.

---

also be cautious in our extrapolations regarding the seven-hundred-year cycle. In the section "A Periodicity of Frenzy," we spoke of the twenty-first century. But the cycle in question is of only *approximately* seven hundred years. It would be a mistake to assume that we will be safe until the middle of the twenty-first century. All we can say is that the hour seems late.

THE CHOSEN PEOPLE
OF HIROSHIMA

On August 6, 1945, a U.S. military chaplain blessed the crew of a plane and wished them a successful accomplishment of their mission—to carry and drop an atomic bomb over Hiroshima.

There was a blinding flash, a hot blizzard and earthquake, a mushroom welling into the sky; bodies charred, tens of thousands of them—and the dawn of the atomic age.

A score of years later (1967) Robert Jay Lifton, professor of research in psychiatry at Yale University, published a very powerful book, *Death in Life: Survivors of Hiroshima.* He interviewed seventy people from among the survivors, of all walks of life. He found little essential difference in the mental make-up among the educated and uneducated, the physicists, writers, preachers and shopkeepers, housewives, peasants and the wayward and the outcast. I quote, below, Paul Goodman's impression of Lifton's book because of the insight at which Goodman arrived:[6]

"They insist—it is seventeen years later—on the abiding presentness of the event. They refuse to betray the sacred literalness of its detail. The event was Great, some could even speak of a 'quicker happiness' in the sense of awakening from the illusions of this world. They are Chosen People. Many have stigmata like marks of the Lord Jesus. They form a mystical fellowship with a mission. They are a sacrifice. They are to be liberators of the out-caste and apostles of peace. They are despised but they are the stone that the builders rejected.

[6] Paul Goodman, "Stoicism and the Holocaust," *The New York Review of Books,* March 28, 1968, p. 15. Cf. exchange of letters between Lifton and Goodman in ibid., April 28, 1968, pp. 36–37.

"One must be morally perfect and not sell the experience to money-changers. Indeed, according to some, any speech and self-initiated or socially-initiated effort are a profanation. One must safeguard purity by refined taboos, e.g., not to wear nylon stockings for they are made by DuPont. Yet since there has been a reversal of values, it is incumbent on people to 'despoil the Egyptians,' e.g., to operate on the black market. The matrix of human existence has broken down; there has been a wound in the order of being: one cannot live unless there are a new heaven and new earth. 'I saw actual hell in this world.' Traditional religion, Buddhist or Catholic, cannot cope with the new fact. The new dispensation belongs to all mankind.

"But some day the lion will lie down with the lamb. 'They dream . . . that the energy of ten million horsepower per gram be delivered out of the atom into the hands of the people. That the rich harvest of science be conveyed, in peace, to the people like bunches of succulent grapes wet with dew gathered in at dawn.' This Isaiah-like vision is by Sanchiki Toge. A rainbow will shine after the black rain. Even before the Bomb, in the ordinary past, we were not living—it was a delusion; but a man keeps seeing an indelible still photograph of his innocent childhood: it is fixed—until the new world in which to come alive.

"The elect saints, in communion with the dead who are also present because they took part in the real event, are meantime purgatorially trapped in the meaningless interim of current history. Presumably they are awaiting a new prophet who will make possible a transfigured life. . . . While waiting, some sit silent and remember the wrathful theophany; others speak with the dead."

What fixed my attention on Paul Goodman's essay was his insight in comparing the experience of the persistent reaction of the survivors of Hiroshima with the experience and the subsequent attitude of the Israelites of the days of the

Exodus, an event long passed into history; he actually starts his piece by referring to Martin Buber's book on Moses: ". . . the Bible story cannot be taken literally yet is not unhistorical: *something* happened that was, to those people, super-natural or crazy, and the account we have received was their attempt to cope with the experience, to regain their wits, to reconstitute themselves in the world that had been transformed."

This parallel was not drawn by Professor Lifton; he, however, drew parallels with the mental evolution or, rather, mutation in the survivors of the Nazi camps. A major portion of *Death in Life* deals with "defense-mechanisms against trauma: repression, denial, reaction formation, blotting out . . . screen memory, scapegoating and alibi-ing, self-hatred in order to avoid the anxiety of abandonment, identification with the power that has harmed one in order to avoid the anxiety of impotence, turning of anger against the self and becoming guilty."

The book re-creates "a remarkably total traumatized environment," but the reviewer is critical of the pathological prognosis of Professor Lifton. To me, however, the mental structure—because it is not merely an attitude, but a permanent posture—of the *hibakusha* (by which name are known the survivors of the holocausts of Hiroshima and Nagasaki) is a revealing and meaningful phenomenon in the light of events long past, in this confrontation of "a fragment of sanity in a bland storm of madness" with "the people of the world against the Powers of the World."

Lifton writes: "The survivor's major defense against death anxiety and death guilt is the cessation of feeling. In our observations on Hiroshima we spoke of this process, in its acute form, as psychic closing-off, and in its more chronic form as psychic numbing. I would suggest now that psychic numbing comes to characterize the entire life style of the

survivor."[7] The "psychic numbing" among the survivors of
the catastrophe is, in my view, the first stage toward a submersion of large parts of the perceived events into a partial
oblivion. The basic dissimilitude of the two events—the phenomena of the days of the Exodus and those of 1945—is in
the fact that the former were not of man's making and they
were global; the events of our time were man-made, and
while they were also global in the sense that the war spread
to all the continents and seas, they were epitomized by the
burning of two cities in the release of "energy of ten million
horsepower per gram." For the people of these cities the catastrophe was nothing less than global and only later did
the survivors learn that they were selected from all other
cities for that experiment in overkill. But before they
learned this, it was for them no different than if all cities the
world over had tumbled. The experiences of Hiroshima and
Nagasaki frightfully mirrored the moments when "in the
morning watch the Lord looked unto the host of the Egyptians through the pillar of fire and of the cloud" (Exodus
14:24).

OF THE ROOTS OF ANTI-SEMITISM

In *Ages in Chaos* I have exposed the untruth of Manetho's
identification of the Israelites with the Hyksos. Manetho
was an Egyptian historian of the third pre-Christian century
writing in Greek. The hatred that until then was directed
against the almost legendary Hyksos, the early conquerors
and exploiters of Egypt, was from then on directed against
the Jewish people. I showed also that the Hyksos, known to
the Egyptians as Amu, were the same as the Amalekites of
the Bible who dominated the Near East, as well as Palestine,

[7] Lifton, *Death in Life*, p. 500.

during the long period of the wandering in the desert and of
the Judges; I quoted numerous old Arabian authors who
describe the conquest of Syria–Palestine and Egypt by the
Amalekites and the domination of Egypt for four or five centuries by the Amalekite dynasties of kings. The mode of exploitation of Egypt by the Amu as described by the Egyptian sources, and of Palestine by the Amalekites as described
by the biblical books, was identical; and, most important, it
was shown that it was King Saul, the first king of the Israelites, who succeeded in terminating the Amalekite rule by
capturing their stronghold, el-Arish, which is but the ancient
Avaris, together with their last king, Agog.

The Jewish people harbored a deep hatred of the Amalekites from the days of wandering in the desert, where
the former, tired and thirsty, were mercilessly pillaged by
the Amalekites, through the days of the domination by the
Amalekites and Medianites who would regularly invade the
country with their numerous cattle before the harvest. This
hatred was kept alive not only through all the centuries of
Israel's and Judah's life in their own land, but also through
the long period of their diaspora, or world exile, down to our
days.

The Jewish historian of the first century of the present
era, Josephus Flavius, accepted Manetho's identification of
the Israelites with the Hyksos, and by that time the anti-
Semitism of which Manetho three centuries earlier was the
first known literary source had already spread in the ancient
East. To rectify this wrong I have in *Ages in Chaos* followed
the correct identification by a short discourse on the beginning of anti-Semitism.

There may be another aspect besides this ancient misidentification.

Since antiquity the Jewish people have claimed that the
great catastrophe of tribulations, destructions and paroxysms of nature, as exemplified by plagues, the parting of the

sea and the vanishing of the pharaoh with his host, was caused for the benefit of the sons of Israel. Egypt was punished because of harshness toward them; the Israelites were spared during the visitations of the plagues; their leader called upon Egypt the plagues and upon its armies the waters of the Sea of Passage; the Israelites were the beneficiaries of the cataclysmic events. It is of lesser importance, or of no importance, that historically they were not spared by the raging elements as the biblical story claims they were, and midrashic sources to the opposite effect were cited in *Ages in Chaos:* at the plague of darkness only two out of every hundred Israelites survived, and at the Sea of Passage many of the escapees were engulfed by surging waters. The story as described in the Bible and as believed by the Jews and by other peoples of antiquity and of modern times is and was important: when Egypt suffered, the Israelites were exempt from the tribulations, and they gained their freedom from the slavery of many generations.

The natural catastrophe that visited Egypt visited the entire terrestrial globe, and many places on it went to complete perdition. The experiences of those days persevered in the collective unconscious mind of the human race.

These conceptions—whereby the Israelites were thought to have been the only ones spared from the catastrophe of the days of the Exodus, and Manetho's misidentification of the Israelites with the Hyksos—are at the root of anti-Semitism, which persisted through the centuries.

THE SLAVE TRADERS AND THE SLAVES

The continent of Africa is divided into what is called the Black continent, and the northern fringe, north of Sahara, occupied by the Berber or Arab states. The east coast of

Africa runs parallel to the west coast of Arabia, and on the Indian Ocean coast, Zanzibar, the old station of Arab slave traders, completes a wide arc. The Arabs preyed on the African blacks and sold them into slavery wherever there was a demand. Slavery was also imposed on war prisoners of other races, and Columbus made slaves out of his Carib prisoners, but it was, especially in modern times, the continent of Africa that served as the hunting ground for slaves. From the beginning of the sixteenth century the importation of slaves into the Western Hemisphere was uninterrupted until only a few generations ago: though limited by legislation in the States about 1800, the trade went on till the end of the Civil War and continued in neighboring countries. In 1873, only a little over four generations ago, of the 1,500,000 population of Cuba, 500,000, or a third, were slaves.

Under the heading "Mohammedan Slavery," the fourteenth edition of the Encyclopedia Britannica narrates (and though encyclopedias are not sources I like to quote, I make an exception in this case):

The central Sudan appeared to be one vast hunting ground. Captives were brought thence to the slave market of Kuka in Bornu, where, after being bought by dealers, they were, to the number of about 10,000 annually, marched across the Sahara to Murzuk in Fezzan, from which place they were distributed to the northern and eastern Mediterranean coasts. Their sufferings on the route were dreadful; many succumbed and were abandoned. [It is reported that] "any one who did not know the way" by which the caravan passed "would only have to follow the bones which lie right and left of the track." Negroes were also brought to Morocco from the western Sudan and from Timbuktu. "The center of the traffic in Morocco was Sidi Hamed ibn Musa, seven days' journey south of Mogador, where a great yearly fair was held. The slaves were forwarded thence in groups

to different towns, especially to Marrakesh, Fez and Mequr-
nez."

The sultan levied an *ad valorem* duty on the slave trade.
From Morocco, French, Portuguese, British and other ships
carried the purchased slaves to their destinations.

The Zanzibar Arabs on the eastern coast of Africa were
the greatest traders of all. Black villages would be put to the
torch when their populations were asleep—sometimes with
the connivance of the village chiefs—and the fleeing blacks
would be captured, thus becoming human merchandise.
Many of those transported in chains on Arab ships, often not
seaworthy, died of maltreatment, thirst, and exposure to the
sun, and of some cargoes crossing the Atlantic not more
than fifty out of a hundred survived the passage.

The British, the French, the Portuguese and others buy-
ing the slaves in African markets moved them to Europe—
but mainly to the Americas. The British statistics had it that
exclusive of the slaves who died before they sailed from
Africa, 12½ percent were lost during their passage to the
West Indies; at Jamaica 4½ percent died while in the har-
bors or before the sale, and one third more in the "sea-
soning."

The Zanzibar traders could not claim an equally "favora-
ble" survival of the human cargo.

The slave trade to the Western Hemisphere continued
after the Civil War, but, diminishing, it looked for other out-
lets; with further decline after the 1870s, the chief absorbing
market became the Arab countries themselves and especially
the Arabian Peninsula, the delivery area being the north-
eastern and eastern coasts of the African continent. There
was also an inner trade with the black kingdoms of Uganda,
Benin, and Dahomey, the Arab traders being here, too, the
suppliers; many of the slaves were also sacrificed in pagan
ceremonies. The nineteenth-century explorers, Dr. David

Livingston, Sir Samuel Baker and Dr. Heinrich Barth described these practices.

Black slaves were until quite recently bought and sold in Arabian markets, especially on the Arabian Peninsula. With the spread of the Mohammedan religion among the blacks of the eastern coast of Africa, the traders posed as missionaries, inviting the faithful to embark on pilgrimages to Mecca. On arrival they were sold, never to return to Africa to tell the true story of their travels. In the littoral kingdoms, in the emirates and sultanates of the Arabian Peninsula, slavery was sanctified by tradition and protected by law, in violation of declarations of principles made by the European powers at various times, notably in the latter part of the last century. These notwithstanding, several member countries of the United Nations still practice slavery at home.

A characteristic social and psychological phenomenon is taking place in the process of the black reawakening in the United States. The fourth- to tenth-generation descendants of slaves (in the case of the West Indies only the third generation) feel a resurgence of the longing for Africa that accompanied the fettered slaves on their forced voyage to this country and haunted the thoughts of the first generation of those working on plantations or in mines. But together with this back-to-Africa sentiment, a strange, even pathological phenomenon takes place: the most militant among the American blacks look to the Arabs as their allies and mentors.

The descendants of the slaves return to those who preyed on them, took them captives, chained them, drove them mercilessly across deserts, let them die from thirst exhausted at oars on galleys. The urge to return to the tormentor or to his descendants, to adopt their religion and to hail them as saviors is a reaction for which psychology knows the cause: a victim's children remain fascinated by the one who wielded a whip over their father.

EXPLOSION OF POPULATION

The explosion of the world population is proclaimed by many as the greatest danger to the future of the human race, a peril not of a distant future but of the next two generations. I remember when the population was 1.6 billion human beings; now it exceeds four billion, two World Wars notwithstanding. Calculations are being made as to what the human population of the world will be on the basis of the present increase: something like seven or ten billion at the end of the century. Not in the bomb explosion but in the population explosion lies the greatest danger, proclaim many sociologists and almost all population-growth experts. The populations that already verge on starvation multiply the fastest. The teeming people on the shores of the Ganges live at the lowest standards: homeless, they defecate in public squares, in the open; they sleep on the streets of Calcutta; and they procreate—cohabitation is one of the few pleasures left to the penniless and unskilled. At the same time sacred cows—all cows and bulls are sacred to the Hindus—wander uninhibited, devour crops, and even when they die a natural death are not permitted to be eaten.

In Egypt, the population of fellahin (farmers) in the Delta, one of the most densely settled areas in the world, suffers from malaria, from trachoma (an infectious eye disease that leads to blindness) and from bilharzia (a hookworm which bleeds the kidneys). With the major part of the inhabitants of these places thus suffering from one or more of these debilitating diseases, the population increase, for the entire Egypt of thirty million, is still over two million annually—the major share belonging to the Delta.

The planet—our common home—is not growing; its food reserves are limited and already insufficient to feed all the people of the globe, and the cry is heard again—as it was a century and a half ago, when Malthus first wrote—that the growth of a population outstrips the growth of means of subsistence. And as for food, the ocean does not yet deliver its full potential share: what is presently being taken out of the ocean is only a fraction of what is available. In any case lodging, education, transportation—all these also present problems increasingly difficult to solve should the lowly of the earth be lifted from the dust and mud and require such facilities.

There are those who proclaim the doctrine of the sacredness of human life in all circumstances. The most callous murderers are fed at public expense for life or for the duration of sentence as the case may be, the death penalty having been abrogated in many states. Abortion, even of a child conceived in rape, was until recently a punishable offense in many places—and it has already happened that the rapist and his victim both serve terms in the same penitentiary, only the rapist, being guilty of a smaller offense, soon goes on parole; but the victim stays behind bars for the murder of the unborn child.

No program of relief from the dangers of population explosion is offered here. But possibly the significance of the rapid increase in the world's population lies elsewhere than in concern over food. Let us consider the phenomenon as to its possible sociobiological significance.

In the animal kingdom those forms of life that are in danger of annihilation usually produce the largest number of progeny. Insects that have to endure the inclement winter multiply enormously so that at least some of the progeny will survive and perpetuate the species.

With this process observable in many animal forms on land and in the sea, the great explosion of population in the years following World War II requires close attention. It is quite possible that there exists a regulating mechanism. It has been observed since ancient times that during and following great wars, the birth of males is definitely greater than the birth of females—nature acting as a regulator. And if nature can—by means unknown to man—switch the birth rate in favor of males, cannot the same nature regulate the very increase of population to protect the race from impending extinction?

If it is so, then the seemingly uncontrolled increase of population is a symptom in an incubating stage of a dangerous illness.

ARMAGEDDON ON THE DRAWING BOARDS

The editorial elucidation in the New York *Times* (December 18, 1974) of the Vladivostok agreement between the leader of the Communist party in the Soviet Union and the President of the United States reads:

> The new accord would permit each side to build a "first-strike" force of new MIRV multiple-warhead missiles, a minor portion of which could threaten to destroy the bulk of the other's silo-based ICBM's, while the bulk of the attacker's force remained in reserve to deter retaliation. Neither side has such a capability now. . . .
>
> The Vladivostok agreement would permit the Soviet Union, starting next year, to replace with new, bigger, more accurate MIRV-tipped rockets virtually all the ICBM's it is permitted under the 1972 SALT I accords—1,320 of its 1,410 silo-based missiles. Before 1985, its present 1,410 warheads would go to an estimated 6,700. With their large size, this is more than *three times* the number of warheads needed for a "high-confidence" strike at the United States' 1,054 ICBM silos.
>
> The United States, under the Vladivostok agreement, can replace all its first generation Minuteman III and Poseidon

MIRV missiles—800 of a programmed 1,030 already deployed—with bigger, more accurate Minuteman IV and Trident I missiles. It plans, in addition, to add 288 larger Trident II missiles aboard 12 monster Trident submarines at a cost of almost $1.5 billion *each*. With this program . . . the Joint Chiefs of Staff reportedly are confident that they could beat the Russians to a "first-strike" capability by two or three years.

A nuclear "Pearl Harbor" with its unforeseeable consequences would not be initiated lightly by either side, of course. But the existence of this capability on both sides during a future crisis—and the massive advantage it seems to offer for the side that shoots first—raises possibilities almost too horrendous to contemplate.

Crisis instability—the penultimate danger of the nuclear era, second only to the ultimate horror of an actual nuclear exchange—clearly has been brought closer by the failure at Vladivostok to limit MIRV missiles to low levels.

. . . Without MIRV, an attacker must fire at least two missiles at every opposing silo for high confidence of success, thus disarming himself more than the enemy. With MIRV, the attacker has the edge. One missile carrying six warheads could destroy three enemy ICBM's.

The editorial goes on with more figures and calculations—or miscalculations. Armageddon is on the drawing board.*

The basic unconcern over what would follow if, or more properly when, the accumulated thermonuclear weapons fly out of silos, or out of submarine vessels, or out of orbiting satellites—this unconcern is a psychological phenomenon of no mean significance. The acquiescence amounts almost to a desire to have the doom come. Do not the churchgoers ask for the Second Coming, and do not business concerns distribute to their shareholders profits from merchandise of

* With the deterioration of the situation in the years since this editorial was written, these observations acquire even more meaning.

death, and do not superstates together with "developing nations" live in anticipation, and is not the morbid disconcern but a rejoicing in such anticipation? To consider others being annihilated on a grandiose scale fascinates so greatly that it is worth the risk of the same. Or will only the sinners have their eyes gouged out, the teeth knocked in, the skin peeled off, flesh burnt, and spinal column broken?

The SALT agreements are but a license to augment and refine the arsenals and bring order into the chaotic business of the rush toward turning this globe, eight thousand miles across, into a salt plain of Sodom.

Chapter VI

DREAMS AND HALLUCINATIONS

TO OPEN A DOOR

I pose the question: Would the reading of my books and the absorbing of their contents alleviate the pressure caused by racial memories existing in all of us? Proper psychoanalytical procedure is violated by revealing all at once instead of making the patient arrive at his insights gradually. This is only one of the violations. But there is a great advantage over the accepted procedure in that instead of working on the assumption that the dominant traumatic experience of the human race was in Oedipal and castration experiences, the true traumas are laid bare.

Is it then true that the making known of events forgotten but enshrined in the collective subconscious mind can only arouse hostile attitudes? If this is the case then my work is pregnant only with hatred and irritation that will surface, leaving the repressed contents where they are. In their exposure phobia, the repressed contents in us would lock the escape window of the collective psyche from the inside.

There must be a potent disturbance agent in action at the reawakening of repressed hereditary amnesia. It happens also with individual psychoanalytic patients that an untimely disclosure causes a breakdown of a schizophrenic nature: in the hands of unskilled analysts such results must not be uncommon. In my psychoanalytic practice I have established a preventive procedure and never failed to follow it. I will digress here and briefly explain my approach.

The narcissistic tendencies must be treated first, and as long as these tendencies prevail, the latent homosexual inclinations or the Oedipal ties should not be the subject of analytical work. It is by a successive advance into these less pathological regions in the psyche that the analysand has the chance of liberating himself from autistic eroticism, the stage at which the ego is nearest to a schizophrenic disturbance. Should the analyst tackle the hidden homosexuality first, he would, by bringing such component of the neurotic personality into his conscious mind, make an escape from autism no longer possible; and should the Oedipal complex in autistic or homosexual patients be the first target of the analytical work, the autistic as well as the homosexual tendencies would be cut off from the healing process. The sickest part of the neurosis—the autistic libido—needs to be exposed and treated first; then the homosexual component of the personality would come more to the fore provided the Oedipal tendencies are not made prematurely the analyst's target; the emergence of the homosexual component in an autistic patient would signal an advance in the analysis. Lastly, the Oedipal component is the object of treatment—and with the emergence of that tendency (almost paramount in all patients) into the conscious mind, the last stage is reached in guiding the patient to normalcy. I found that such procedure never fails—in a matter of months only, hardly ever of years—to achieve successful completion of the analysis. Too many analysts, unaware of the proper procedure, drag the analysis on for years, and what is worse, occasionally lose their patients to schizophrenia: the advance in the proper direction is blocked, and the premature tackling of lesser deviations sends the patient in the direction of greater deviations by locking doors that need to be kept open.

In the right procedure it is as if a door of a ward of greatly disturbed patients is opened and the patient is given a chance to move into a ward of less disturbed, and, again, by the same stratagem, into a ward of the least perturbed, before leaving the hospital; whereas tackling the Oedipal complex first in patients with emotional disturbance in the stages of homosexual and autistic fixations is equivalent to locking the door leading to the less-disturbed ward and leaving open only the exit into the wards of the more and more disturbed.

Freud intuitively followed the correct procedure but nowhere formulated it in his writings; the art of analysis being that of art *and* of science, not all—by far not all—analysts follow the rule; and then endless analyses or, what is worse, devastating results, not without cases of suicide, are the fruits.

These rules of cautious procedure I pursued, with gratifying results, in my analytical work; but in having presented my understanding of man's past in the frame of a reconstruction of the historical past of the planets, I lost control over the effects, often greatly perturbing, on the psyche of individuals exposed to that revelation.

BEDLAM'S BASEMENT

I have repeatedly heard and occasionally read that in the hallucinogenic state produced by peyote and other such drugs violent sensations of impending doom, of cosmic encounters, of ensuing pandemonium, overcome the novice or the habitual user. The vividness of the experience and the terror it evokes cause such physical phenomena as runaway heartbeat, shivering and excessive sweating. By no means does such a state always result from intake; it is claimed by those who have studied the matter that only when, under the influence of the drug, a very deep stratum of the subconscious is reached does the terror that lives in every one of us come into the open. From one such observer who experimented on himself and on scores of individuals ranging in age from fourteen to seventy-four (to do so without coming into conflict with the law, he moved to Mexico), I received this description:

". . . From the most deeply buried levels of human experience, appear vivid and terrifying recalls of what must be the basic engrams of the human race—the series of catastrophes suffered by this planet. Bits and pieces of these basic engrams have occurred in many sessions for many subjects, even in the first session, but for a long time we were not able to understand what was occurring. With the release of some of the charge, so to speak, the recalls began to become more clear and coherent. Catastrophe memories have appeared clearly in some twelve or more sessions involving a number of different subjects, and what is felt and described forms a different pattern from anything else which we have encountered.

"All such memories are loaded with terror. There is usually a continual violent shivering and shaking of the body, sudden sensations of heat followed by intense chills, much confusion and a sense of utter disorientation, sudden shock-like reactions and convulsive spasms, as well as visual images of electrical discharges, high winds, torrential rains, earthquakes and an indescribable pandemonium of noises."

Having read the minutes of one of such sessions, complete with every word uttered by the person, partly in response to the prodding of the experimenter, and with the detailed description of the torture-like experience of a groaning and utterly frightened subject of the experiment, I inquired: But why does a person look for such an experience? To this I did not receive a satisfactory answer from my correspondent. Is

it, then, a matter of the need to revisit the time and the
scene in which man and beast tried in a supreme effort and
with dwindling success to get away alive from a collapsing
stage, the dimensions of which were the whole Earth and
space besides?

A teacher in the public school system in the city of New
York wrote me a letter in which he told of his dreams, of his
hallucinogenic experiences, and sounded his alarm at man's
inability or unwillingness to view his heritage. He expressed
his thoughts almost poetically—they looked on paper almost
as if they were written in ancient characters of biblical
Hebrew—yet they were written in modern English. He
wrote:

"You have begun for mankind the dredging up of a past
filled with unimaginable violences. Before the Armageddon
is recreated for us by that substitute-comet idol, the
H-bomb missile, although the race is close we must do everything in our power to remember who we are, and why
we are violent. You have provided ethnic, historical, archeo-
logical, geological evidence for your theories on the holo-
caust-collisions, but you have not tapped the most important
source of truth—the memory of the catastrophes themselves
as experienced by our surviving ancestors and passed on to
their descendants through the dream and hallucination. I
have had hundreds of dreams—some involving the comet-
approaching terror, the flaming, feather-arrow-brilliance
across the sky, the wrenching fear, the attempts to build
shelters, the preservation of food and water, the hopelessness, the raining stones, the burning mutilated bodies,
the endless black waters, the steeples and debris on which
survivors cling, the burning cities, the oil droplets descending, the forced witnessing of charred bodies, the bits of
corpses hurtling through the air, the labyrinths which the

survivors fled into beneath the earth (part of the unconscious obsession of the spelunkers), the fantastic scaffolds
built above the deluge, the flying and soaring through the
air when gravitational forces changed, the obsessive wor-
shipping and propitiation of the violent comet gods, the
goon squads picking the doomed and carrying out of terrible sacrifices, the decimations of other tribes in the name of
comet divinities—the cruel tortures inflicted on those breaking the covenants and comet-cult taboos. How can you
avoid the incontrovertible evidence for the truth of your
findings—namely that all of us are descendants of the survivors—and all of us know the truth (although we deny it
viciously in the face of the depth of the terror and anguish,
and calumniate those who stir the embers of our nightmares
which we hope will 'rest in peace,') except that we are in a
state of shock and universal amnesia, and dare not remember the terror for which mankind blamed itself (as witness the fall of man from the garden of paradise). You are
blasphemed because the hurt is too great for any one mind
to cope with. The hallucinogenic drugs are one way of ex-
periencing the terrifying past without threatening total self-
annihiliation. The alternative of our not being able to re-ex-
perience and re-create from our horror-filled past is a dismal
one: using violence to force us to remember—the violence of
fusion or fission—or perhaps the explosive super-novae chain
reaction scientists are in a frenzy to discover and try out.

Must we re-create the disasters and decimations, the planetary turmoil—or shall we join forces and encourage the recall
of our common origin—and our common loss—through the
re-creation of the historical truth from the material of the
dream as a record of actual events seen from a certain geo-
graphical and emotional perspective? Perhaps we will also
remember man as he was before the idea of sin and shame
made him leave the earthly eden that earth once was, and
which can be vaguely sensed by visionaries, and crudely ex-

perienced by the ingestion of hallucinogens? The terrors of mankind are now emerging, but we shall find them harmless, for if we can face them, we not only find them awesome but exhilarating—the consciousness of mind streaming back into the bedlam basement of Hell brought on by the immense conjunction and commingling of our planet with a fiery dazzling plasmatic comet of immense richness and horror-beauty."

If there is truth in what this schoolteacher wrote to me, it is quite possible that the widespread use of hallucinogenic drugs has as one of its springs the urge to live through the traumatic experience, the memory of which is buried deep in man's mind.

PLANETS IN DREAMS AND ANXIETY

Regimen, a work the authorship of which is ascribed to Hippocrates, the great Greek physician of the latter part of the fifth century B.C. and the early part of the fourth, has a chapter "On Dreams." It contains the following observation:

"Whenever the heavenly bodies wander about, some in one way and others in another, it indicates a disturbance of the soul arising from anxiety."

The translator of *Regimen,* W.H.S. Jones, supplied a variant for the rendering of the sentence "some in one way and others in another," namely, "now in one direction and now in another."

The movement, and especially irregular movement, of the planets in dreams is connected with unconscious terror: Hippocrates' observation and interpretation are based on a deep insight. But why should great anxiety find its expression in dreams, a product of the subconscious mind, by making planets wander in the sky, if the celestial bodies have always moved on regular courses, never threatening our planet and its inhabitants?

To illustrate Hippocrates' description of a fearful dream, with planetary bodies leaving their paths, I present here a dream narrated to me by a professor of history at a Midwestern university when, on the occasion of a lecture I gave there a few years ago, a group of faculty members entertained me with a meal and conversation:

"Some time ago you expressed interest in a dream of mine that I recounted in the course of a dinner table conversation. The dream took place, to the best of my recollection, when I was six and a half or seven years old (i.e., late 1920 or in the course of 1921). . . . In the dream I was in the yard of our house late at night; with great awe and fear I watched the heavens where there was no moon but where the heavenly bodies, larger than normal, swarmed 'angrily' or contended with each other. The words I weigh very carefully to suggest the impression that was actually made.

"The dream made a particular impression on me because the press at the time carried reports of prophecies of the 'end of the world.' Later (a year or so) when I obtained a library card I spent quite a bit of time reading into children's books on astronomy. At the end of my undergraduate work at Harvard I almost decided on a career in astronomy when I was offered a fellowship on the basis of my work as an assistant at the observatory there. I cite all this in partial explanation of why the dream persisted in my mind. In the course of the thirties the dream was forgotten. In the spring of 1944 I recalled it in conjunction with my witnessing air raids on London but also in conjunction with my reading of J. W. Dunne's *Experiment with Time,* which suggests that in sleep the mind is released to travel through the fourth dimension. (Dunne, a mathematician, had some vogue in England at the time.) Naturally the thesis suggested that my childhood dream was a pre-visit to wartime London. However, strictly speaking, the dream was different from the night air-raid in that in it the swarming heavenly bodies filled the sky and were unrelated to activity on the surface of the Earth. There was nothing like the searchlights, the rockets or anti-aircraft fire."

In the case described here, the dream and the anxiety and curiosity it provoked directed the studies of the dreamer in his college years and almost decided his choice of profession.

We saw in an earlier section that Jung developed the theory of the collective unconscious mind. Beside one's own private subconscious, in every one of us lives racial memory: we are carriers of some characters—Jung called them archetypes—identical in all humanity. How these patterns came into existence Jung did not know; he only believed he knew that these archetypes are found again and again, as patterns of thought and imagination, and he ascribed them to the primeval emergence of man as *homo sapiens*. It did not occur to him that common and terrifying experiences, in which all participated and from which few survived, engraved themselves in man's inheritable substance. After Jung's death quite a few of his disciples started to see the answer in the events described in *Worlds in Collision*.

Shortly before his death, Jung described a dream that had been reported to him:

. . . As the sphere very swiftly approached the Earth, I thought at first that it was Jupiter that left its orbit, but as the sphere came closer, I saw that despite its large size, it was far too small for a planet like Jupiter. . . . As we realized that it must come to a terrible collision with the Earth, we felt well-understood terror; but it was a terror in which awe dominated. It was a cosmic act that called for awe and wondering. . . . A second sphere and a third one and more approached with great velocity. Every one of them crashed into the Earth. . . .[1]

Something out of racial memory revealed itself in this dream. Even the first impression that the approaching celestial body was the giant Jupiter, later corrected, represents the great illusion that the forebears experienced at the approach of Venus, mistaken for Jupiter, as described in *Worlds in Collision* ("Zeus and Athene"). The din of crashings recalls the experience of the same time when "mighty thunderings" (Exodus 9:28) accompanied the fall of the meteorites; these noises were no less terrifying than the destructions the meteorites caused.

The near-freeing of submerged and terrifying racial mnemes would naturally produce an expectation of doomsday. In the above-quoted book, his last, Jung prefaced a discussion of flying saucers with these unusual words:

> It is not arrogance that urges me, but my medical conscience which advises me to fulfil my duty and to prepare the few whom I can reach to the fact that events are in store for the human race that signify the end of an Eon.

In these parting words, after over half a century of study of the human mind, Jung revealed his vision of things to come.

TORNADO

In 1966 a violent tornado whirled through Topeka, Kansas, and its surroundings and wrought devastation. In October 1973 a resident of that city of about 100,000 wrote me a

---

[1] C. G. Jung, *Ein moderner Mythus* (Zürich: 1958).

letter on the psychological reactions to that experience by
the residents of the city and by himself. Tornadoes often endanger that city and warning signals are given, and though
he was absent when the tornado hit, it was the reactions of
the inhabitants he observed to the warning signals that
made the writer of the letter wonder. Over a year after first
writing me he wrote again on the irrational psychological reaction, as it appeared to him, comparing it with his own excessive, but opposite, reaction to these signals. Since the correspondent had been, as he described, through analytical
treatment, it was instructive to read even in his first letter
the realization that not infantile impressions and fears, nor
social surroundings and interactions, but some racial experience is the residue undissolved by the analysis of personal
experiences—the very realization at which Freud arrived
after many years of contemplation. The man from Topeka,
however, was not familiar with the Freudian concept of submerged racial memories. This concept is regularly, even con-
sistently, left undiscussed and unattended by analysts in
their work, thus showing that they not only neglect what
Freud himself regarded as his crowning achievement but
are themselves purged only to a certain depth. The fault is
Freud's insofar as he realized the "demoniac power" exer-
cised by the submerged racial memory of a traumatic experience of the past, but failed to realize the nature of that experience.

My correspondent recognized the aversion in men of
science to facing reality, and he did not spare barbs. Not
aware of Freud's insights into the racial memory, he referred
to Freud as having only immersed his toes in waters of profound depth and having withdrawn them as too hot. A better acquaintance with Freud's deeper insight, not communicated to him when he was on the analytical couch,
would have precluded this slighting remark. He had the ad-

vantage over Freud in that he had read the pioneer work of the apostate to whom he was writing. Thus he knew that the traumatic experience of the human race was not in repeated parricide in prehistoric caves, but in the horror of helpless man, who since the beginning of time has more than once been threatened with destruction by hostile elements— elements from which he burrowed in the ground "as a mole" or stampeded to sometimes fatal shelter in trembling mountain caves.

Since the man from Topeka was away from the city during the tornado of 1966, I inquired how close he came to such an experience that he reacts the way he does to warning alerts. He describes, in reply, the panicky feeling he felt when caught in traffic in Minneapolis, where he grew up, even in advance of police siren warnings of a tornado. Minneapolis is a city only rarely afflicted by these rotating storms, and others in the traffic responded quite differently from the Topekans who had experienced the event of 1966. In the face of a tornado warning only a few years after the 1966 experience, the latter acted as if trying to negate the experience. A comparison with the reaction of the people of Hiroshima comes to mind, always keeping in view the much greater scale of the event and much greater toll in human life. But the event of Hiroshima was, in its turn, not on the scale of the global events of the human past.

From his letters I could learn that the writer studied law and is a man of some prosaic occupation; neither his training nor his qualifications would make him an expert in the matters about which he wrote. Yet the analysts of the Menninger clinic near Topeka and with them the entire great crowd of those who, one generation after Freud, sit at the head of the couch and listen "with the third ear" should consider whether there is possibly any lesson to learn from these missives that I shall extensively quote.

"Dear Dr. Velikovsky,

"If I understand your theory correctly, the crux of it is that people repress awareness of whatever frightens them the most and against which they feel helpless. To me, and to anyone helped by psycho-analysis, which I have been, this is a painful truth. But what links my own experience with what you propose, is that once I worked through 'forgotten' early childhood episodes, there was still something left. Something far more terrifying than all the rest. So abhorrent is this thing that associations have led nowhere. But slowly the nature of this beast revealed itself. . . .

"I live in Topeka, Kansas, a place notorious for its unpredictable, violent weather. Prior to my psycho-analytic impasse, the weather bothered me when it got bad, but it wasn't something I worried about during more pacific intervals. Yet even then there was a sense of foreboding, of imminent evil, when the sky darkened. My analysis kept bumping me against this nameless subconscious dread. I developed a great fear of darkness, as if it would definitely bring the greatest of catastrophes. My instincts when outside are to cover my head, and run for cover. The sky has become the enemy. Now taking cover should provide considerable relief from extant storm conditions—with me it doesn't. It's as though these inimical forces threatening me are far too powerful to be defended against. My feelings of helplessness are total and it is this aspect that is the most intolerable. The only relief possible is *rage* directed against anyone, anything, blamable for any reason, no matter how unconnected to the source of the threat. . . .

"I've watched closely the reactions, attitudes, of others in this climate to the approach of bad weather. Seven years ago a tornado did devastate this town, and since then there have been numerous alerts. So, the people pretty much know the odds, the effects, the behavior of such storms. They know, as do I, that with radar and warning sirens, unless you are alone and crippled, safety is assured. Yet when these taut times do occur, almost nobody acts in relation to experience or known probabilities!

"There is either near-panic (as with me), or, far more frequently, refusal to take the warning seriously. This second response, by people who've been *in* a tornado, is the amazing one. I must ask why would people who have survived and know exactly what to do to survive again, not react?

"I answer this, as in my own case: this horrible external event makes a connection with one much more horrible, that in its inescapability actually did render men defenseless. . . ."

Fifteen months later, as the second letter shows, the thoughts expressed in the first letter had not retreated to the back of the mind of the writer, and not only continued to occupy him but also led to some new realizations:

"Dear Dr. Velikovsky,

"For a number of years now, I've been thinking about what I consider to be man's greatest natural enemy. No, not death—worse. I refer to man's tendency to view the world and himself only as it most pleases him. . . .

"Dr. Velikovsky, you are hated, dreaded, because you bring up something basically intolerable. You shatter the control belief. You present a cause for certain human behaviors and feelings, that is *inhuman* in origin, uncaring, and worst—vastly uncontrollable. Inhuman forces, perhaps blind, perhaps tinged with malevolence, surround us. And it is this state of affairs, more than any other, that is unacceptable to the human mind. . . .

"I wrote you a year ago about some observations I'd made concerning tornadoes. These natural events, to me, are things that make a connection with repressed memories of a catastrophic nature.

"I live in Topeka, Kansas, in an area, in spring and fall, under an almost constant threat of tornadoes. In 1966 a tornado struck here. It was half a mile wide, and though I wasn't here at the time, the films taken of it were the most horrifying thing I've ever seen. . . .

"My interest in this subject was spurred by the observation that just a few years after the disaster, people acted as though it hadn't happened. Even now, when warning sirens are screaming, most people do nothing. They refuse to alter their behavior at all. Nor is the attitude one of hopelessness in the face of an awesome enemy. In fact, there is much one can do to protect himself. Listen to the radio, head for a basement, pay *some* attention. Yet, many don't even do those simple things. They act as though nothing was happening—almost as though nothing ever *had* happened.

"And incredibly enough, this bizarre response is typical of people who lived through the great tornado of 1966, people who saw, heard, its devastation.

"I must say that there are a few who feel the terror, who tremble and can acknowledge the peril. These, however, often act as though there is no escape, even though the basement is seconds away.

"At any rate, all this seemed most peculiar to me. Especially since I've known people who have been in severe auto wrecks. The response of these people is dramatically different from the tornado behavior. The wreck victims don't see driving as hopelessly dangerous and give up the practice. Nor do they ignore the episode, driving as though nothing had happened. They do continue driving—but more carefully. They act rationally.

"Why, then, the strange behavior under the tornado threat?

"People around here tend not to use the word 'tornado,' preferring the word 'storm.' Quite a difference in the emotive power of the two words. Even more peculiar is the fact that animals seem to *know* when a tornado is likely. The insects disappear, birds stop singing, dogs tremble and head for cover. This does not happen in a mere thunderstorm without tornadic potential. Even I can feel it—the very air holds its breath, waiting, hoping, wishing.

"Everyone feels it, while most completely disregard the information. It's not simply that they have no control—because they *can* get out of the way, they *can* take cover. They don't. And to me, it is rather like walking down a railroad track, seeing and hearing the oncoming train, and not stepping aside.

"But a train seems to be different from a natural menace. People *do* step off the tracks.

"The event is too enormous as it rolls out of the Southwest. Blackish gray, it comes, stretching from horizon to horizon, moving like a gigantic wave. Day becomes night, and you feel—like it's the end of the world.

"It's an outright apocalyptic experience.

"And for that reason, no amount of learning about these storms, no amount of emergency practice, can lessen the horror associated with them. Denial seems the only defense. It is an anesthetic that serves people as emotional protection from the terror."

Less than a fortnight after the date of the just-quoted letter, and in response to my inquiry, the man from Topeka described his earlier experience in Minneapolis: there the residents had no great calamity in their memory, yet in response to a siren, disrupted all traffic. Having reached home he looked up:

"Very high, and a good distance off, I saw what looked to be a thin, grayish-white wisp hanging from the clouds. Its bottom end, still considerably above ground, was moving, almost like a cat's slow twitching tail.

"Though it was going away from where I was, I went into

the basement feeling there was no escape. My reaction was so severe, I feared for my heart. Nothing came our way, but as it turned out, a dozen lives were lost elsewhere in the city.

"The interesting thing about it, was the less than conscious feelings I'd had preceding the sighting. My body *knew*, even before the sirens, that an agony was approaching. It was a sensation I'd never had in any previous storm. It was the feeling of death—not just mine, but everybody's. Again, it seemed, imperatively, like the end of everything.

"I remember something else. When I was a small boy, I was particularly impressed and confused by my father's behavior during storms. By nature he was a very rational, careful person, who never ceased reminding me to be careful about cars, falls, knives, electricity, yet when a storm came up, he would drop whatever he was doing and go outside. Even in severe electrical storms, he'd wander out in the open.

"He showed no fear at all, and was oblivious to all else. And the look in his eyes was very strange. Kind of bright, a glaze, not at all characteristic of the very focused, alert, and prudent man that he otherwise was. It scared me. It was as if he were being drawn, with no conscious participation, into a union with the violence.

"I've seen much that same thing here in Topeka. People who lived through the tornado of 1966 suddenly find things they have to do outside during the sirens. Mowing lawns, going to the store—that sort of thing. Never in a hurry, but slow, languid, detached.

"There was a study done of the survivors of that disaster. Afterwards, no one mentioned what had happened, nothing was said of the destruction, even as they were being pulled from the rubble. Nor did the victims say much about the experience, other than to describe the external activity going on around them as the tornado struck. No subjective accounts, no impressions of how it really was for them, appear. You get the feeling that nothing was really experienced— consciously. Immediately afterward, there was little sign of emotion of any kind. Few describe anything but the state of being dazed.

"One couple I know, who lived only one block from the total devastation, emerged as soon as the thing roared past, got in their car and drove across town to keep a bridge-playing date. This, despite the fact that it took them two hours to negotiate the mile of debris that lay between them and the party. Business as usual, nothing at all had happened.

"Just last spring, with the skies pregnant with malice, sirens screaming, radio reporting a tornado over the city, my neighbor is sitting on his front lawn, his two-year-old son in his lap. He, too, had been in Topeka in 1966. Lightning had just knocked the power off, and split a tree in half across the street. Yet, there he was.

"I don't know if you'll find these vignettes helpful. Hopefully, they convey the frightening incomprehension that is the rule during such times. Perhaps my unconscious is closer to the surface than most people's. They act in accordance with no existing reality."

Chapter VII

A CHRONICLE OF OUR TIME

The entire chapter that follows should be read as a running commentary on some of the events of the last two decades. Each section of the chapter was written at or near the time of the events that it describes, whether student unrest, Watergate or Jonestown. It is for this reason that persons now deceased, such as Mao, or now deposed, such as Amin, are sometimes referred to in the present tense.

MNEMES AWAKENED

What is behind the great shift that, with the young generation in its grip, changes society to such an extent that a zoologist would suspect strong mutants in action, and if a similar shift were taking place in primates or quadrupeds, would emphatically proclaim the arrival of new variants, even of new species? A nineteen-year-old hippie and his middle-aged parent in outer appearances do not appear one and the same species, but in their thinking and behavior they are not even of the same genus. The well-groomed, properly dressed parent is in pursuit of everything his own parent was—advance and achievement in study and profession, procreation and recreation in marital and extramarital sex, comfort and pleasures, golf, a motorboat and a summer house, possibly a Sunday visit to a church; a daily study of Wall Street news; nightly boredom and an occasional escape from it in some swanky eating and drinking place—and overall security and status, status and security.

On the other side of the generation gap a fundamental parting with everything just enumerated—from purpose of life to appearance: barefoot, in torn jeans, with long and unkempt hair on head and face, these being the outer signs of rejection of anything accepted, revered, striven for, or possessed by those on the other side of the gap.

What is beneath this complete change of inner and outer values? What drives young men or women to such a resolute separation from their fathers' and mothers' ways of life and ambitions? What makes them prefer a sleeping bag to a well-sheeted bed? A life with hardly any shelter to a life secured by parental care, in a suburban villa, protected by stocks and bonds?

What causes, then, a well recognizable portion of the young generation to strive in the opposite direction? What is it that makes them reincarnate the caveman in appearance, though even a caveman probably knew to shave his face with flint? A caveman without a club—instead, a flower.

Is it a reawakening of the Essene movement, of which we learned from the Dead Sea scrolls? Are these hippies a religious group frightened by the expectation of doomsday? Do they emulate the early Christian sects by opposing violence?

They *are* frightened. They were running away to some "safe" location at the approach of an asteroid, Icarus, that with its million- or billion-ton mass was expected to nearly cross Earth's orbit in 1968. They have been most concerned —actually in trepidation—at the prophesied possibility—for many of them certainty—of California's slipping into the ocean because of a breaking away along the San Andreas fault, with a sudden and vast enlarging of the fault and a bursting of the Earth's crust. They do not live their lives in disdain of earthly goods, indifferent to life itself. They *are* most concerned with life, even more than their stable, sturdy fathers. They are bitten by something which they know not and which makes them seek an ascetic life. They are frightened and they don't know by what, but the solid ground on which their fathers built is to them a most insecure base, a place to flee.

It appears that, born of parents who lived, and some who fought, in World War II, and of grandparents who lived and some who fought in World War I, the new generation looking back into a past filled with violence senses the approaching doom.

A man who wished to lead human society to peace devised the original formula underlying atomic weapons—and destruction; before him, the man who invented dynamite established a yearly prize for peace: which of the contradicting endeavors of each man prevailed?

Therefore, pessimism grips those who are about to enter their adult life; but the conscious realization of the possibility of a holocaust, a realization built on twentieth-century history, is not the entire story: something in the unconscious mind of human society began to make itself felt. Something provoked it to half-awakening; a throb in the arteries, a hidden key to the endocrine system, the solar plexus, medulla, gray matter—wherever the ancient terror had dug itself in, something started to vibrate slightly differently, the key made a partial turning, some mnemes lit up, a spark flying forth and back and around the million cells holding the engrams of racial origin—a network crisscrossed by flashes.

In the Sistine ceiling painting by Michelangelo, Adam is awakening as an outstretched arm with an extended finger reaches to meet his hand. But it is not a flying bearded man attired in robes, a God father, who awakens Adam. The call

is from within, from the unconscious mind, from a racial submerged heritage—deep, unfathomed, yet ever-present, never
eliminated in a single human being or a single animal species. The ancient engram required a chord sounding in uni-
son with it. The two World Wars, the ashes of Hiroshima
and the cinders of Nagasaki touched such a chord; then the
story of ancient cosmic upheavals needed to be told so that
the lost phylogenetic memories could come forth with sails
unfurled from the sealed haven they entered thousands of
years ago.

LATE 1960S: STUDENT UNREST

University campuses grew malcontent and soon turned
into scenes of violence. Presidents and other administrators
were locked in their offices, furniture and laboratory equipment were smashed, archives were dispersed or thrown
through windows, or burned; entrances to public rooms
were blocked, police were fought, barricades were erected.

Student unrest has been sifted by many authorities for
causes elusive and explosive. Some said it was motivated by
political issues, by left- or right-wing causes, by militant
pacifism, by integration problems, by sex, its license and
deviations; others said that it was a manifestation of nihil-
ism, of hippies' distaste for orderliness and regulation, of
teenage drinking, mass drug addiction, or of a religious upsurge. What force, then, was really behind the unrest?

It was motivated by all of the foregoing, but more than
anything else by students' realization that in a new age of
man, as different from the over-stayed Victorian age as that
was from the neolithic, they are being instructed by inadequate methods, from antiquated textbooks, by teachers
whose recognition of a new era in sciences and humanities is
often discernible only in a feverish pursuit of grants.

Wherever I have gone at the invitation of college and university groups I have found the students and the more thoughtful of the faculty appalled by the inadequacy of the training offered, in an era when man has already burst the frame of his tiny world with its petty rivalries and has taken the first steps into a larger cosmos, having only one score of years earlier released the energy of the microcosmos.

The science of several decades ago, perpetuated in college textbooks, is full of outdated views bequeathed from the nineteenth century. The college teacher, with few exceptions, is an authoritarian because of his inner insecurity and frustration. Fossilized notions are offered as ultimate truths eliminating any need for further probing and thinking.

Geology is taught according to uniformitarian principles laid down long before oceanographers and students of paleomagnetism discovered evidence of global violence in recent time; in astronomy, newfound knowledge of interplanetary magnetic fields, electric charges on the Sun and planets, and plasma in space is kept out of most college textbooks—or referred to only in prefaces; the high heat and retrograde rotation of Venus, gases escaping from a Moon long thought to be cold to its core—such anomalies carry no explanation in the astronomy taught in the colleges.

Disquieting news arrives in an incessant stream from arctic regions, from the bottom of the oceans, and from archaeological sites around the world, and in disturbing data from radiocarbon-dating laboratories, from paleomagnetic studies, from paleontological finds.

It is already sensed that the theory of evolution built on the Malthusian principle of competition for means of livelihood producing new characteristics in species—the only mechanism offered for the evolutionary process—is divorced from the truth. The coming of entirely new forms of life is just a few decades away, practically around the corner, with all the agents—radioactive, chemical and thermal—necessary

to change the animal and plant kingdoms already available
for the task to be performed—in the laboratories, one hopes,
not in a nuclear holocaust with attendant degeneration.

The house of knowledge, stable and everlasting only two
decades ago, is now all torn by fissures, with walls bulg-
ing or caving in, foundations removed from under the structure, roof collapsing. Ancient history, anthropology, social
sciences, philosophy, and psychology, all of them experienced tremors and shocks and collapses, though the care-
takers of these domains too often pretend that the old values
are inviolable. In front of these structures the guardians pretend that all is perfect inside; where a disagreement exists,
there is an apparent agreed partition of the territory among
the competing proponents. In psychology, for example, adherents of "schools" swear by their chosen masters, having
made no progress in a generation, unconscious of the ines-
capable need—or unwilling—to face at last the issue of racial
memories.

Evaluating new scientific theories presents problems for
the power structure within the scientific establishment, with
a few hierarchs clamping lids tightly over the jugs of fer-
ment and inquiry; the scientific press serving a policy of
keeping the general public and even the scientific community in ignorance of the interdisciplinary significance of
newly discovered facts; the chorus of grant distributors and
grant recipients, a self-perpetuating upper crust, living off
science and honoring its great ones by naming college build-
ings and institutions after them; the students who sense that
they are distracting their professors from "projects" and
from soliciting funds, and from writing the reports on funds
spent and more needed; the teachers in the humanities—
C. P. Snow's "other culture"—envious of scientists and strain-
ing their brains for ways to formulate a fat project with a
meager idea; "thinkers" scurrying from coast to coast and
from foundation to foundation; the retreat of brains from

teaching to industry; the publication of half a million "scientific" papers each year, most of them intended to justify grants and promote promotion. Boards of trustees, themselves a crop of prep-school alumni, Sundays in pews, Mondays to Fridays on direct lines to Wall Street, appoint chancellors and deans and disappoint all others.

In all this pandemonium, two or three million students in the United States alone, many of them burdening family resources to gain the benefits of higher education, are told to write weekly papers, to submit mechanically to written examinations, and to keep up their grades. Helplessly caught up in the stream, losing individuality, they are molded into report writers and graded punch cards, with the ultimate prospect of cap, gown, diploma and all, and a license to enter the race, but only at a pace slower than that of the instructors themselves trotting behind those who precede them in the procession.

How not to rebel?

DISMAYED AND CONFOUNDED

The rebellion of the young was full of hope—the millennium was about to begin. The hair was grown long, John the Baptist was imitated in appearance, but the rebellion was against asceticism as well as against materialism; regulations were to be violated, young and not-so-young flocked to "rapport psychology," which struck out Freud and the rest of the "schools"; orgies were practiced as curriculum in some campus classrooms as the call came for tearing down all inhibitions.

Pot and acid, uncombed hair, colorful patches on torn trousers, four-letter words filling belles lettres—and the vision of John the Baptist turned out to be a Halloween mask. With knives and shotguns young girls massacred rev-

elers unknown to them, on the stages cohabitation was
played nightly, Christ was feted as superstar; but the millennium loomed farther away than ever. The movement ran out
of momentum; a circle came full and once around and full
again and there was no exit from the purgatorium; the aura
of a decade earlier was no longer a sign of a millennium but
of decadence, a signal for parting with all values. Drug
pushers claimed to be modern prophets; the naïve and the
innocent sucked into the whirl looked longingly for a true
prophet, and there was none in the cathedra and none in
the pulpit and none in the woods. The maimed in Vietnam
were received back by the society that sent them as if they
were lepers, were turned away from all doors, the drug
addicts among them even from veterans' hospital wards. At
the "crossroads of the nation" flashing signs advertised horror pictures and homosexuals peddled their services.

The "new left," anti-Semitic and with many Jews in its
ranks, keeps pointing toward the other superstate, the Soviet Union. But the other superstate is a house of de-
tention. The news media there are censored and for decades
now have printed only the dullest resolutions of production
quotas, and writers are told what to write. Writers who
deviate are put into prison; twice Nobel-prize-winning authors were thrown out of the literary institution and called
scum of the earth. In Z, a film about happenings in Greece,
shown to uncounted millions, the Russians export their art
to Greece—the Bolshoi Ballet—but the Americans export
atomic weapons; the Greek organizers of a demonstration of
protest against atomic weapons are mauled and the permit
for a public meeting is revoked. In Soviet Russia, however,
no such permit would ever be asked for or given. Seven
brave men who one day assembled on the huge Red Square
to demonstrate for liberties were sent to psychiatric wards,
this being the new punishment for dissent, whereby the gov-

ernment avoids the embarrassing situation of holding trials of people whose only crime is unconventional thinking.

Then where is the land of promise? Are the eight hundred million blue ants, all lifting the little red book with the thoughts of Chairman Mao, free beings? They may believe that they are, but they are not—one brain serves for all of them.

In their agony, the young, in a land where the Constitution permits deviation, try it in all directions, but finally find themselves disoriented and leaderless, confounded and dismayed.

MAN LANDING ON THE MOON

Man's eternal dream is to go to heaven alive; an urge to cast off the shackles binding him to the rock of his birth and to soar and touch with his mortal body one of the planetary gods or goddesses; a longing for a visit to paradise without first going to the grave, and without passing through purgatory; ascension while alive, like Elias who went up in a chariot of fire (or was consumed in a ball of lightning), but with a return to Earth; to participate in the banquet of gods. . . .

It was a long way. What a drive from times barbaric, a jealousy buried in the genes of a biped envious of the avian family—eagles and hawks, even lowly sparrows; a prince of creation born without wings, looking longingly at caravans of migrating birds: they can soar; he was born to crawl. He bound sails to his back and glided, falling and dying. But then he broke that barrier and surpassed the birds—not yet in 1903 at Kitty Hawk when a glider supplied with a motor lifted and carried him for nineteen seconds, but a few decades later, when fleets of huge metallic birds went on to carry millions of passengers across the continents and the oceans. The ultimate goal, however, stayed always the same: heaven itself.

Soon after the first Sputnik went into orbital flight, Laika and Belka, dog passengers (the raven and the dove of the Noachian ark), preceded man in ninety-minute travels around the globe (an improvement over the eighty days of Jules Verne's hurried land and sea trek). Soon the first man was sent into orbit and the message came from a Soviet astronaut: "I have not seen God there." Then were the laws of nature that made his flight possible decreed by the wizards of technology who sent him off the ground?

When in December 1968 the Apollo 8 crew was circumnavigating the Moon, one of the crew read to all the awe-stricken earthlings who followed their flight: "In the beginning God created the heaven and the earth. And the earth was without form, and void; and darkness was upon the face of the deep. . . ."

Seven months later another crew was on a mission to touch the Moon, plant human feet on her, bring back of her divine body—of a goddess of all ancient creeds. The entire population of the Earth with access to television watched Neil Armstrong step on the Moon, and man—all the family of man—felt a supreme achievement: no longer true were the words, "Earth is the lot of man and the heaven is the Lord's."

But Armstrong and Aldrin, stepping on the Moon, knew that they did not come to a banquet of gods: the banquet hall was a most desolate landscape of pits and strewn stones, with a black sky over them, and no sound—even if one shouted, even if mountains burst and lunar strata slid. The astronauts performed a ritual dance and left the Tranquillity station strewn with their refuse—the descent module, some instruments and a plastic flag—a Salvador Dali phantasmagoria.

Reverse of ancient values: the hell is now above, the paradise below! The good Earth is enveloped in white clouds through which blue seas and green land are visible, yielding to yellow deserts, and brilliant ice caps, a jewel of creation from which man succeeded in lifting himself to another world—a world utterly desolate, a reminder of what could have happened to the Earth, an echo of the submerged racial memory that must have carried through generations the vision of the days when the Moon was "confounded" and man's ancestor was overwhelmed by terror.

Man stole rocks from the Moon, lifted himself from it and found in the vastness of space the mother ship and returned to Earth. Crowds mobbed the astronauts—they escaped the fate of Prometheus who brought fire from the sky and was chained to a rock in the Caucasus, a vulture feasting on his liver.

The vision of ancient terror—man wished to forget it: on the second day of the returning flight one of the astronauts inquired—and the whole world could hear—"What's the trend on the New York stock exchange? Stocks and bonds?" Being told that stocks and bonds were lower, he resigned himself by observing that one cannot go to the Moon without some punishment.

The President of the United States promised a rock apiece to all heads of friendly governments on Earth. The scientists who came to see the quarantined stones were all too eager to persuade themselves that the catastrophe that befell the Moon took place earlier than her association with the Earth—a lullaby with which the Earth science since Aristotle has soothed man's awareness of the great events his ancestors witnessed.

But the unawareness, sanctioned by the neo-Aristotelian view, is also the cause of man's wretchedness. At the time that Apollo 8 with its three men, the precursor of Apollo 11, was circling the Moon in December 1968, ambassadors at the Vietnam peace conference in Paris spent days, and then

weeks, discussing the shape of the conference table, preliminary to the beginning of any negotiations. At the time of
Apollo 11, men—same genus, species and variety—bogged
down in swamps, still fought a senseless war. If the three
men had perished on their lunar voyage, how deeply be-
reaved the human family would have felt; but fewer than
one hundred Americans killed in a week in Vietnam—
besides the maimed—was something almost to rejoice in; for
many weeks not so negligibly few had met their death.

In Biafra, hundreds of thousands starve; in the Middle
East, hundreds of millions of Arabs from Morocco to Iraq
and the Sudan besiege a small and dedicated remnant of a
race that—counting dead and alive—was never for the last
three thousand years a minority in Palestine; on the Ganges,
hungry human masses carry on a wretched existence; in the
waters of the oceans atomic submarines scurry, ready to
send out thermonuclear missiles on populated cities; and in
the vastness of Siberia two supernations prepare for Armageddon.

PAGES FROM A NEWSPAPER

Two days of newspaper reading—even only a paragraph
here and a paragraph there—and the implications for the
palpable future of the human race grew alarmingly threatening. The President of the United States negotiated in the
capital of the Union of Soviet Socialist Republics with its
leader concerning the limitation of the atomic weapons race
—and all that was achieved was to agree on the limitation of
the defense of civil population, but not the limitation of the
development and manufacture of the atomic warheads, at
least not for the ensuing eleven years. I told this to the first
man I chanced to converse with that day. "Is it possible," he
exclaimed, "to leave the population unprotected, while an

unbridled race for more and more developed atomic warheads is going on?" He thought I erred in my reporting of
what I read. I did not err.

"I would understand an agreement on the development
of protection for the civil population while desisting from
creating more powerful and more sophisticated weapons of
annihilation," he said as if reading my thoughts. But, as we
have learned, there is no logic where both sides negotiate at
a table under which is an abyss—where both sides are basically irrational. Man as a species is irrational, and those most
susceptible to the atavistic urge for self-destruction have
only a thin skin over their lust for kindling a global holocaust.

The newspaper reports: Soviet Russia has atomic weapons of more formidable thrust; the United States has developed multiple warheads superior to those of the communist
arsenal. And the communist camp insists on a prolonged period of unrestricted development of multiple-warhead missiles.

The infant and the young are heading toward a simulta-
neous charred death; and I cannot help remembering the
stench of burned horseflesh in a stable that I, at that time
probably four years old, was brought to see a few days after
a fire.

Another item is almost happily presented to the readers of
the newspaper: in a few years there will be two dozen
members in the atomic bomb "club." Richard Nixon on a
quasi-peaceful and triumphal visit to the Middle East promised an atomic plant to Egypt; India, which received pluto-
nium from Canada for peaceful purposes, recently exploded
an atomic bomb, while Indira Gandhi, still professing that
the atomic plant is solely for peaceful purposes, promises,
according to another newspaper item, soon to explode a thermonuclear bomb. The majority of India's population of 600
million is near starvation; poor and wretched and hungry,

many without a roof over their heads, stretching their ema-
ciated, shriveled arms for a handful of rice—against the in-
congruity of prestigious entrance into the most expensive
and exclusive "club." In a few years it will no longer be exclusive. Another greatly overcrowded land, Egypt, is jubi-
lant at the prospect of atomic plant and fuel and bomb. By
what reasoning, then, should Idi Amin, the Big Daddy of
Uganda, have been kept out of the "club"? Amin, who employed sledgehammers to crush the skulls of those who came
into disfavor: should an opportunity to initiate a "big bang"
be denied to him, if the membership in the club be extended
to two dozen?

The generation is also without a prophet, or singularly
poor in leadership; there is nobody to whom to listen; a generation of advanced technology, with nobody of ethical stat-
ure whose voice should be compelling. Former generations
had such leaders. Alexander Solzhenitzyn saw the iniquity
on a grandiose scale, with human beings dehumanized by
the dictatorial state in inquisition chambers, in prisons, in
slave labor camps, in mental institutions. But the cure he
saw was in a return to the mystical Slavophile movement—
Russia as a third Jerusalem, a rural society, as if material
civilization is of the devil, as Leo Tolstoy, latter-day
prophet, felt in his final years.

On television, about the time of the release of the news
from the Moscow summit conference, the American viewer
was accosted by the spectacle of a young, sixteen-year-old
guru who had just taken a bride, with "God" written over
his head and throne. This is not only not considered blas-
phemy, but donations to him are deductible and his income
is tax-free, as is normal in the United States where, by constitution, state and church are separated.

"You never had it so good," exclaimed the President.
"You are the most prosperous nation." Some senior citizens
changed in their eating habits to dog and cat food, their

dollar—put into savings bonds, as was their patriotic duty—losing its value by the day, almost by the hour. Keep turning the newspaper page. Another small item: department stores suffered two-billion-dollar losses from shoplifting in a year. Statistically, divided by the number of people in America, this figure makes every one of us, infants included, a shoplifter of ten dollars' worth of goods a year. Recidivist rapists are being set free on their own recognizance or given suspended sentences by order of the courts. What President does such a country deserve? The atom button is at his fingertip.

THE FIRE GATE

For two years the United States was in the throes of political scandals known collectively by the name of Watergate. The nation was baffled, even stupefied by the unbelievable disclosures. Watergate was all about a man who made it all the way to the uppermost rung of the ladder, and then held tenaciously when the support began to crumble and finally went down in a descent to which history knows hardly any precedent.

The question is: if Dick was so sagacious that—starting as a delivery boy in his parents' little neighborhood grocery store, who gratefully thanked customers for a nickel tip, he outsmarted Tom and Harry and everybody else and eventually saw a procession of kings and presidents seeking his favors at the White House—how could he be also so unreasonable as to perform in a way that made the majority of the nation despise him, after all his achievements on the global scene? How could he be so self-destructive as, having ordered a widespread net of spying, also to have installed bugging devices to spy on himself? And if he wished to stand

194   MANKIND IN AMNESIA

great before posterity, why did he also record the foul words
with which his language abounded?

The outraged nation follows, all enrapt, the tale of the
inanities conceived in the White House by the President or
his agents and executed in burglaries and other acts out of a
cheap spy movie: secret rendezvous of conjurers plotting on
park benches, in hotel lobbies and darkened cars; a suitcase
of hot money hidden in a railway station locker; contra-
bandist flights to Mexico, with a melodramatic episode
thrown in of a faithful secretary who tripped over a tape re-
corder, causing extensive erasures. In those months, the
President again and again faced the cameras and assured
the nation that no wrong had ever been done by him or his
staff. Why, then, did he not destroy the incriminating tapes
as well?

When finally the roof of the White House was in effect
blown off, a man with a drooping chin descended from the
invisible throne of the Oval Office and, surrounded by his
household, spoke to the nation, sounding as if he were again
the grocery boy: he spoke of his saintly mother and of his
hardworking father. He still did not appreciate the bewitch-
ment of the mightiest man on earth, up to the day before,
going past the doorman and as a last gesture, as it appeared
to me, raising his arms in a victory signal before being lifted
by a helicopter from the lawn. It was no comedy; it was all
tragedy. Possibly in years to come a more penetrating trage-
dian—an Aeschylus, a Sophocles, a Euripides—will recognize
what it was in the man elected by the nation that triumphed
over him, and caused him to act irrationally. What was the
spell that outsmarted him, his logic and his cunning?

What is the answer to the riddle?

Whatever Nixon's personal shortcomings, there is a factor
that needs to be considered, without which perspective is

lost. It was lost to Nixon himself, but this is in the analytical nature of things: a man does not take into account the most obvious factors when he tries to figure out what dominates him, what hits him.

Entering the White House as President and as Commander in Chief, Nixon was entrusted by the nation, even by the entire Western world, with a detonator that could incinerate the people of the globe. This trusteeship is a responsibility of the President alone, twenty-four hours a day, three hundred sixty-five days a year. An atomic attack provides a very short time for warning; listening devices are positioned in the north, in case an attack comes over the pole—the route is shorter and warning time is less—and in other strategically placed stations in America and abroad, and they are monitored every single second, incessantly. But it is the President who has the fatal decision to make, possibly on the spur of a moment. Stations encircling the potential enemy, in Europe, the Near East and Far East, have their retributory missiles ready for instant command.

The President fulfills all kinds of official and ceremonial functions and lives his family life as well. But whatever he thinks or does, he must be cognizant of the trigger entrusted to him, and of the siloes from which intercontinental atomic warheads can be fired in retaliation in this balance of terror, and of the atomic submarines stealthily cruising not far from the coast. He cannot keep all this out of his mind, not even in sleep, even if he is not consciously thinking of it.

A fateful power like this was never before vested in a mortal. A reader of the gospel description of Gehenna, where the sinners are thrown for damnation, should imagine that he alone is entrusted with the key to that place harboring uncounted progeny of Adam. He can open the pit and let the people out, or he can add more sulfur and fire; and this reader, if he can visualize it, should also contemplate

how this preoccupation would permanently dominate his activities.

The fear of committing a mistake, an irreparable mistake,
the extreme strain—such as came into the open in the confrontation between Kennedy and Khrushchev in the days
of the Cuba ultimatum, or, to a lesser degree, in the days of
the alert following the Yom Kippur War—the gnawing feeling of being inadequate to the task of guardian of human
destinies—all this never for a single moment leaves the trustee of the cosmic power of destruction.

A sense of suspicion of everyone and even of oneself must
take hold of the human possessing the facility to terminate
history, at least the history of civilization. Irrational acts will
be committed, almost by compulsion. When papers were
stolen from the Pentagon and the theft was traced to an em-
ployee, who supplied them to the press and thus also to the
potential enemy, he could have been apprehended without
a burglary of his psychoanalyst's office, a deed for which
Nixon took the responsibility but which he did not know
how to justify. And every other step showed fear and suspicion: the actions directed from the White House under
Nixon have the stamp of a personality suffering simultaneously from the mania of grandeur and the mania of persecution, two manias that usually go together. The grandeur
was not imaginary—it was intrinsic in the role; nor was suspicion out of place, if plans exist at this very hour to incinerate instantly two hundred major American cities. But the
suspicion contorted judgment and the Watergate scandal
resulted—possibly because Nixon was more perceptive than
Johnson before him or Ford after him.

A basic fact needs to be recontemplated: being descendants of the survivors of great paroxysms of nature of the
past, we are possessed by the urge inherited through racial
memory to repeat the violent performance. The brain cells
of the man in the position to call down the cataclysm must

be like over-taut strings, intoning in his consciousness a strange tune.

The danger of the President's possible mental derangement before his exit was sensed by the responsible functionaries of the Defense Department, and as newspapers reported, the Defense Secretary made secret temporary arrangements to preclude the President's exit coinciding with ruin by the pressing of the button. Did not the first Secretary of Defense, James Forrestal, in 1949, with the button there at his finger and with Soviet Russia not yet possessing a comparable nuclear arsenal, run out one early morning hour into the street of a Florida resort crying in panic that the Russians had invaded the United States of America? He was a man of exceptional abilities. The heritage of racial fears, the Freudian urge to re-create the traumatic experience of the past, the unconscious Promethean struggle between the urge for destruction and the urge for survival—and James Forrestal hurled himself from the window of a high-rise military hospital, to find peace with himself.

Lyndon Johnson, whose motto was, "Let us sit down and reason together," misled Congress and the nation by staging the Tonkin Bay incident and then vastly increasing the involvement in Vietnam. He sent nearly five hundred thousand young Americans to a country in which the United States had hardly an economic or political interest, the very name of which was unknown from the school days of those sent there to kill and be killed, to maim and be maimed, to burn out with napalm the fifteen-year-old Vietcong draftees, and themselves to be drowned in swamps and lost in forests they defoliated. Johnson mortgaged the next generation's wealth to pay for this agony, actually a surrogate for the great atomic carnage.

Atomic weapons carry a danger of radioactive fallout; but amassed and before they are ever used, they carry a different kind of fallout—a disturbance in the brain cells of the person responsible for their use or nonuse, who has the fuse always with him along with a not easily controllable urge to light it.

Extricated from this responsibility, divested of his power, Nixon raised his arms as in a victory signal—but he did not know what he greeted with the gesture.

In San Clemente, in the walled-in Casa Pacifica, the former President wrote his memoirs. He did not know the true line of his defense. So he repeated the blunders of a prisoner-exile on St. Helena of a hundred and fifty years ago, who, after having plunged Europe into bloody wars with horse-drawn cannons, wrote a story of his life as he saw it, or as he dreamed it up, much of which the historians consider untrue.

THE THREE GIANTS

The three giants of our time—the United States, Soviet Russia, and communist China, though unequal in technology and population, dominate the world and threaten its survival. They emerged to their present positions only in this century, actually following World War II. Despite many wars in the last thirty-five years these three have escaped, till now, an all-out confrontation among themselves.

At the end of World War II, America was already in possession of atomic weapons, Russia not yet; and when Germany and Japan were defeated, relations between the Americans and the Russians became strained, some geopoliticians in Washington recognizing that the world domination attempted by Hitlerian Germany would soon be the goal of the Soviet state. They felt that with the Russians earlier or later acquiring the skill to produce atomic weapons, the potential threat of Russia to America and the rest of the world grew larger with every passing day. The strain caused by the feeling that time was being irretrievably lost showed itself when two Americans, husband and wife, were found guilty of transmitting to Russian agents some rough designs. President Eisenhower refused clemency and let them as traitors die in electric chairs while surges of conflicting patriotic and humanitarian emotions tore the nation apart.

The Einsteinian formula—energy equals mass multiplied by the velocity of light (in vacuum) squared; Lisa Meitner's secret, carried by this Jewess fleeing Nazi Germany; the alchemist act on the campus of the University of Chicago, performed by Enrico Fermi, who had left fascist Italy for the United States; the great explosion over the New Mexico desert, a work of many, orchestrated by Robert Oppenheimer; and then, the blinding light over crumbling Japan when the Americans had already repossessed the Pacific strongholds and the Russians belatedly entered the war in the Pacific.

Einstein's verbal reaction was as short as his formula: "Oh, veh!"—a centuries-old Yiddish cry or whisper.

Oppenheimer, who had headed the team that built the atomic missiles dropped on Hiroshima and Nagasaki and on Bikini Atoll, the latter free of men but not of animal life, grew remorseful. The Russians were already much advanced in developing atomic bombs. Edward Teller, who left his native Hungary before the Nazis' onslaught, was at the head of the campaign to develop thermonuclear weapons, and, realizing that the Soviet Union would also develop them, almost single-handedly carried the project through, despite the vehement protests of the vast majority of nuclear physicists, headed by Oppenheimer, as well as the bulk of the scientific establishment.

China greeted her entry into the twentieth century with
the Boxer Rebellion. The largest nation in the world, long in
the clutches of exploiting colonial powers, and as late as
1932 still a prostrate and defenseless body against Japanese
expansion, China emerged after the mid-century as one of
the three superstates in the world. England, against whom
Kaiser Wilhelm II warred in World War I, was the greatest
power at the beginning of the century; Germany, which became a world power when all the colonial dominions were
already shared out (as Leon Trotsky put it), emerged from
World War I as an empire on relief; and of the Great Five
of the time between the wars—England, France, Italy,
America and Russia—only the last two could claim that status thereafter, though Russia lost twenty million people in
World War II, again as many in the civil war and through
starvation, and for a third time in Stalin's purges.

China went through the expulsion of the Japanese army,
the "long march," internal rift, the flight of the Kuomintang
to Formosa, the exile and annihilation of the kulak farmers
and the structuring of a monolithic state under Mao, a disciple of Stalin, now in rift with the Soviet communists.

In the materialistic regime Mao became supreme: his
work, wisdom itself; his body, in his rare swims across the
Yangtze River, holy to perceive and divine to touch. Con-
fucius was thrown from his pedestal into the dust, his teachings outlawed.

Stalin, torturer and killer of millions, who spoke Russian
in a heavy Caucasian accent, who started as a seminarist in
a theological service in Tiflis, who when in power closed
churches and made Stalin-worship—"Stalin, our sun"—a religion of the state, was not free of fears and remorse. Some
nights he would drive to the cemetery in the yard of the
Nove Devitze Monastery on the outskirts of Moscow to
kneel at the grave of Aliluyeva, his wife who took her own
life, leaving him a daughter, his only child.

Tortured by fear and suspicions, his death in his own bed saved the group of doctors whom he had accused of plotting to poison him.

The Soviet Union, having dramatically preceded the United States in space travel—Khrushchev with his broad grin at the Americans for sending an orange-size, minuscule probe, while the Russians were sending heavy, two-ton ones —felt that the time had come to bring atomic offensive power as close to American shores as the Americans had in Turkey to the Russian border. The Cuban confrontation followed, and, risking an atomic war, Kennedy made Kosygin back down and remove the offending weapons.

China had not yet developed anything comparable to the Russian atomic arsenal. Mao and Chou En-lai turned China and its cities into an underground net of passages built to serve as shelters when the inevitable war with Russia would take place, with Russia attacking with atomic weapons. China prepared to lose several hundred million people out of its eight hundred million, but determined to survive and invade and take over Siberia, which is almost empty of population, as otherwise China is doomed to starve, with its population pressing against deserts and unproductive lands. As of today a million Russian soldiers occupy positions along the Russian–Chinese frontier, the Amur River.

I will interrupt this narrative. I let the story develop without my interjecting psychological insights—let it not be another psychoanalytic hour. Yet pausing at this point I ask the reader, what would he make of the following?

The five-pointed star—the ancient symbol of the planet Venus—adorns the headgear of every American, Soviet, and Chinese soldier.

GUYANA MASS SUICIDE

On November 20, 1978, newspaper headlines made known the mass suicide of the cultists of the so-called People's Temple, led by Reverend Jim Jones. The initial figure of nearly three hundred suicides grew in daily dispatches from Jonestown, Guyana, as more and more corpses were discovered, to more than nine hundred. The cultists had followed Jones, their undisputed leader, first from Indiana to California, then to Guyana, there to die in a ceremony in which over three hundred children were also sacrificed, given poison to drink. In the orgy of human destruction, death was not all self-inflicted: many were shot by other cultists.

Psychologists and sociologists had little to offer in efforts to explain what had taken place. The cultists lived under the spell of the personality of a man who had some ideas of social reform; he amassed a fortune in the millions by making his followers transfer to the commune chest, of which he was the sole dispenser, their possessions, in some cases selling their homes. He demanded complete submission to his will: some of his abusive sexual practices—such as performing a homosexual act on a male member of the cult in the presence of women—were described by those few who survived self-annihilation. He acted also as if he were an incarnation of Jesus. He was suffering paranoia—that much the psychologists could tell—but what was at the source of this disruption of personality, and what lay in the deeper strata of the psyche of the cultists who were attracted to him, some of them from highly cultured backgrounds? What made them follow him into the jungles of Guyana, one day to extinguish their lives, leaving their bodies, with children, even infants, spread mostly face down, dressed, some holding their arms around others, in groups, but also some alone, stopped in apparent efforts to run into the jungle? There must have been a panic, engendered by the panic in their leader. Beyond this nothing could be offered in explanation, but this explanation required no degree in psychology. It was obvious to all who saw the scene, if only in newspapers or on television, and certainly to all who visited the site in the jungle.

Before a fortnight passed, paperbacks were feeding but leaving unsatisfied the curiosity of those who wished to understand, possibly fearing to find in themselves something of the same urge. I admit to having read, very cursorily, the news releases with their evaluations. My daughter, Ruth V. Sharon, a psychoanalyst, brought me a photograph published in the newspapers of Jones's "throne." What made her give me this picture was a sign in large letters behind the throne. It read: "Those who do not remember the past are condemned to repeat it." This sentence originated with the Harvard philosopher George Santayana, and I used to quote it before my audiences on the college campuses, usually concluding the terminal section of a lecture—the section regularly dedicated to the theme of mankind in amnesia.

Jones was living in terror, and this terror he also partly conveyed to those who followed him. The social reforms, the oriental despotism, the hoarding of money, the persecution complex, the sexual malpractices, all were efforts to bring to the surface something that was not given to release. If he could he would have plunged all the living to their deaths.

To contribute to the understanding, a fathom deeper, of the agony of the false messiah of the Guyana jungles, and of his human herd, I will quote from a book, *The Pursuit of the Millennium,* by Norman Cohn, published in 1957. Several years ago a reader of mine, Cathy Guido of Binghamton, N.Y., then a student, by now a lawyer, copied page 144 from this book in the belief it might interest me. It tells of a sect founded by Konrad Schmid, who lived in the fifteenth century in Germany:

> In order to be received into the sect a would-be member had to make a general confession to Schmid, undergo flagellation at his hands and take an oath of absolute obedience to him. From that moment onwards the only obligation which he recognised was total submission to the messiah. Schmid taught his followers that their salvation depended upon their attitude toward himself. If they were not "as soft and yielding as silk" in his hands, if they showed the slightest striving after independence, they would be handed over to the Devil to be tortured both physically and mentally. He was their god and they must pray to him, addressing him as "Our Father."

Those who read of Jones's way of introducing new members into his cult cannot miss finding similarities. The continuation, again, shows Jones's precursor acting as a messiah, who had precursors himself:

"Those who were faithful to Schmid had their reward. They could rejoice in the certain knowledge that in and through them human history was attaining its true end." So we anticipate some roots or affiliation with earlier figures and practices. The followers of Schmid considered ". . . the flagellants of 1349 as standing in the same relationship to them as John the Baptist to Christ. Indeed Christ himself was no more than their precursor; for, granted that he had pointed the true way to salvation by enduring flagellation; it was only those who beat themselves who could claim to pursue that way to the end." And ". . . just as Christ had changed water into wine, so they had replaced baptism with water by baptism with blood. God had indeed kept the best wine for last—it was nothing else than the blood shed by the flagellants."

The following sentence carries the story, unknowingly to its author, another fathom deeper and closer to its historical genesis, because the author of *The Pursuit of the Millennium* next says of the adherents of Schmid's sect:

> These people were convinced that as they beat themselves an angel named—surprisingly—Venus watched over them. Their skins all red with blood seemed garments for a wedding-feast, the skirts which they wore during flagellation they called robes of innocence.

What Norman Cohn apparently regarded as unexplainable and termed "surprising" is not surprising to the readers of *Worlds in Collision*. What appears unreasoned is not so at all.

Over the brooding Jones, and over the command to swallow cyanide, was also a star of disaster, unexplained and unexplored. The human herd was stricken by a panic with which the leader infected them, but to which an ancient terror added its impetus.

LIVING BY THE BOMB

On the last of May, 1978, when newspapers in the United States as well as abroad featured graduation ceremonies on college campuses, and at the same time a United Nations special session on disarmament, leaderless and listless, dragged out the hopeless issue—not even of disarmament but only of limitation of armament—a citizen, L. C. Bohn, published a letter in the New York *Times*. I reproduce this letter:

> If it does nothing else, the U.N. special session on disarmament should remind us what an artificial and precarious world we have made for our children.

This is the season when we tell our new graduates to be positive about their future: to work, to love, to live life to the fullest, be a credit to themselves and their country, raise families of their own, and perhaps to leave the world a little better place than they found it.

But the sorry fact is that the world we are offering these shiny new graduates teeters on the edge of catastrophe. The chance of nuclear war in any week or month or year is tiny. But no one can live a life in a year. Most of those who have thought about the facts agree that over a period of 20, 30, or 40 years the odds favor all-out nuclear war.

By the mad choice of some future Hitler, by mischief at lower levels or in some nuclear-armed Sarajevo, by escalation of conflict in Africa or the Mideast, or by sheer accident, the real future of the new generation is more than likely to be death in war, or dismal struggle in the aftermath of war. Which of our children is prepared for this? How many are planning careers devoted to improving the chance for peace? Which of them is ready to live out his days maimed, burned, irradiated, or blinded? Which knows how to grow food in the wilderness or survive in irradiated rubble? How many have the equipment or skill to tell if water or soil or crops or rusty food cans are safe, or can be made so? Which is ready to move away (to where?) or to dig a hole and live in it, perhaps for months or years; or to diagnose a fever or heal an open wound in his wife or baby? Which of them is ready to organize his fellow survivors for a new start at civilization—or to sink to the life of a savage, preying on his fellow beings and being preyed on by them.

In the absence of thoroughgoing nuclear disarmament, to assume a future of peace is obviously naïve and unrealistic. As things are now, nuclear war is likely to be the event of the age, that shapes the lives of our children to the core.

But we hardly treat it as a core problem. Two-thirds of the people now alive have never known a world without nuclear threat. The very concept of a world without poised nuclear missiles and warheads grows dimmer each decade.

Practically all "serious" people in Washington and elsewhere regard a nuclear-free world as simple-minded pap suited only for politicians' speeches to the U.N. Even the professed, working objective of SALT is not the elimination of nuclear terror (called, of course, nuclear deterrence), but' its "stabilization."

As I see it, we have a choice. We can be "hit" psychologically and stirred to our cores and moved to serious action about nuclear war and nuclear arms now, as a matter of top priority in our public policy and private lives. Or we can expect to be hit physically, in five years or 10 to 20, by the bombs and missiles that we and Moscow have so ingeniously amassed for our "defense."

Nuclear terror—nuclear deterrence—means living by the bomb. Perhaps it will be only just if our generation, which has chosen that path, also dies by the bomb. But our children?

I reread the passage starting with the words "As I see it, we have a choice. We can be 'hit' psychologically and stirred to our cores. . . ." Am I not too late? Do I prepare here a postmortem diagnosis, or a warning in time?

I remember the months and weeks before World War I started. I remember also the months and weeks before World War II started. Once more, familiar sentences, identical words, the same throbbing in a few tuned to apprehend the approaching disaster, and the same apparent insensitivity in the great majority of their contemporaries. I have already reached four score and three. My most unpopular message I have kept too long within me. The psychological "hit," when delivered, needs time to "stir our cores." In the analytical vocabulary a psychological time fuse is called, depending on the form it takes, resistance or projection, and if it is carried on too long or it protests something too important, it may degenerate into the splitting of the personality or depersonalization. Resistance can take innumerable forms: it can manifest itself in an inability of communication, of talking or doing, in misjudgment, in missing opportunities and omitting and neglecting obligations. In projection the emotions are directed against me—a lightning rod.

For twenty-eight years now, before the eyes of the generation now retreating to make room for the next, a psychological time fuse has made the scientific community go through all the facets of self-degradation in order not to face and not to let others face what was our common past.

EPILOGUE

A believer in Providence may think that the human race is "chosen" from all the populations of the planets of this solar system because this race survived the paroxysms that convulsed the family of the Sun. A disbeliever may gloomily contemplate the abysses at the rim of which our ancestors frantically kept hold, with feet sliding and hands losing grip. But alone we are, and our destiny is now to a greater degree in our hands than in the hands of the unchained elements: the elements are well chained, but we are, to use a biblical phrase, "confounded and dismayed." I have undertaken to write this book because of the grave responsibility I feel, as a historian and psychoanalyst, against keeping to myself the realization at which I arrived, that mankind lives in amnesia of its generic past.

The enemy is time. I conclude with a verse that is not my own, and I do not render it exactly—but the hour is late and I will repeat it:

> We are in a race with the Reaper
> We hastened, he tarried, we won.

I hope that it will be that way, and not the other way around.

ABOUT THE AUTHOR

Immanuel Velikovsky, a citizen of the world, was born in Russia in 1895, studied natural sciences at the University of Edinburgh; history, humanities, and medicine in Moscow (M.D., 1921); biology in Berlin; the workings of the brain in Zürich; and psychoanalysis in Vienna. As a young scholar, he founded and edited the "Scripta Universitatis," a collective work out of which grew the Hebrew University in Jerusalem.

Dr. Velikovsky practiced psychoanalysis in Palestine for more than a decade (and later in New York). Eugen Bleuler, in a preface to Velikovsky's article "On the Energetic of the Psyche," wrote (July 18, 1930): "The ideas of the author appear to me very much worthy of consideration. I, too, came upon very similar, in essential aspects quite identical, concepts." Sigmund Freud wrote Velikovsky that he was in complete agreement with Bleuler and that he, too, had independently formed his own opinions on the subject, "which come very close to yours and which, indeed, in some parts quite coincide with them." Wilhelm Stekel described Velikovsky as "an eminent representative of the medical psychology . . . an idealist of the first order." And later, to Chaim

Weizmann, as "one of the most highly gifted of psychotherapists."*

Dr. Paul Federn said in 1947 that Velikovsky was "a genius—a great man. Excellent psychoanalyst—have sent him some of my most difficult cases."†

In 1939 the Velikovskys came to New York and then moved to Princeton in 1952 where he lived until his death in 1979. He is the author of six previous books—*Worlds in Collision, Earth in Upheaval, Ages in Chaos, Oedipus and Akhnaton, Peoples of the Sea,* and *Ramses II and His Time.*

Kronos, a quarterly journal of interdisciplinary studies, has featured articles by Velikovsky and studies of his work. It is published at Glassboro State College in Glassboro, New Jersey.

* Quoted in Ronald W. Clark, *Freud, The Man and the Cause* (New York, 1980).

† In a letter by Lawrence Kubie to Clifton Fadiman. Dr. Federn was chairman of the Vienna Psychoanalytic Society.

INDEX

DATE DUE

7/31/91			
JUL 2 0 1994			
DEC 0 1 1996			